A CONSPIRACY to LOVE

Living A Life of Joy, Generosity, and Power

By River Smith

This book is dedicated to my great-grandmothers Bertha Parker, Maggie Murphy, Chayah Baylie, and Julia Montenaro. It is dedicated to my grandmothers Anna Brezinski and Minnie Bell Walling. This book is dedicated to my grandchildren Caroline, Tom, and Suzanne.

This book is also dedicated to the Pettit Kids, Rosie, Millie, Al, Lena, and Fred, Who tried so hard.

Copyright 2009, C. River Smith

All non-original material utilized under the fair use doctrine. All rights reserved. Copying of original material is encouraged, as long as author is informed in advance.

Satyagraha
LiberationBrew.org
11206 Clifton Boulevard
Cleveland, Ohio 44102
216/651/1302

THE FIRST STEP IS SIMPLE:

Be Generous with Yourself;

Be generous with Others.

Simple, yes.

Easy?
Not Necessarily.

IN THE BEGINNING *there was JOY*

CREATION THEORY

If there is a beginning, I know it is flooded with joy.
Why is it so hard to believe   if there is a design,
that it is etched in love, thrown on a wheel of possibilities,
bathed in a brew of pleasure?
Why else would our skin be so large and receptive to ecstasy
if it's not our destiny?
Why else would our souls sing so loudly
when we stumble upon each other?
Why else would our muscles long for the deep touch
waiting in the fingertips and strong hands of a
brother-sister-lover?
Why else would our ears hear the music,
our blood feel the rhythm of every beating heart,
            every pit of pattering,
as the rain smacks the window,
      the leaf,
                  our beautiful faces?

So much is about
Openings:

Open windows,

Open doors,

Open hands,

Open minds,

        Open *hearts*.

OPENING THE DOOR

And the more I know, the less I understand/All the things I thought I'd figured out/I have to learn again/ I've been trying to get down/to the heart of the matter/ But everything changes/ And my friends seem to scatter/ But I think it's about forgiveness.
Don Henley

So, now that we have a few of the answers, perhaps it would be useful to figure out what some of the questions are. What do I need to make me happy? How do I live a life filled with love and satisfaction? What does it take to not worry so much? How do I gain more power over my life? What does being generous have to do with anything? What can I do to feel more worthwhile?

This book is designed to look at these questions and more. This book is designed to help you explore and challenge. This trail we travel together will unfold before us as we move deeply into ourselves, into the culture that helps form us, into our faith, into our spirituality as we forage for what will sustain a life of *transformative* power. The hills may challenge you, the views inspire you, the journey reward you with understanding that will make the ingredients you possess more useful, and give you new ones to create a delicious and fulfilling feast of life.

To create solutions for our lives right now…. Requires two things of us:

That we do something different than we are doing today, which is just another way of saying we must walk into the unknown;

And that we be different than we are today, which by definition means that we risk separating from others.

Frances Moore Lappé & Jeffrey Perkins

How often I found where I should be going only by setting out for somewhere else.

R. Buckminster Fuller

THERE'S

JUST

NOT

ENOUGH!

How can I be happy when I don't have enough love in my life? How can I be happy when I don't have enough good health in my life? How can I be happy when I don't have enough money? When I don't have enough friends? Enough time?

At any moment in time on our journeys, there will always be things we can identify that are lacking. It doesn't take much effort for most of us to come up with something we don't have enough of. We've been taught that we live in a world of scarcity, rather than abundance. Most of us believe there's not enough, and many of us believe *we*'re not enough. As we think of what's missing, however, in that same moment, there will also always be something we have, something we possess, and the good news is that we have the choice to center ourselves on either what we **don't have** or on what is actually there, **actually present for us in that moment.**

In this moment.

Not long ago a client was speaking to me, telling me that her life seemed cursed. She thought maybe her dead, abusive husband was reaching up from the grave to control her. "Anything that can go wrong is going wrong."

I asked her to give me examples. "Well, I tried to get a job, and the day of my interview my cat got sick, and I couldn't go. I tried to take the cat to the vet, and my car wouldn't start. I got it checked and it's going to cost me almost $300.00 to get it fixed."

I asked if there was anything else. "Of course there is. My brother was going to help me with finances this month, but now the IRS is auditing him. Every relationship I've had since Jim died, I've ended up getting hurt. I had to give our dog up, and she got killed three months later. My son tries to help me move the last time, and he injures his back, and then loses his job because he can't work. My friend agrees to give me a ride to the doctor, and she gets in a car accident on her way to pick me up."
"Anything else?"
"Isn't that enough? My life is cursed!"

If rain doesn't fall, corn doesn't grow.
Yoruba proverb

"Yes, that's more than enough. Those are certainly some very unfortunate incidents that create a lot of challenges." I asked if she would spend a few moments with me brainstorming things that could have gone wrong but didn't.

So Marge and I sat there listing things like:
"My cat could have died.
My car could have been totally broken.
My friend could have been hurt in the accident."
And so on.

It was important to be realistic in listing because those issues must feel as legitimate as possibilities as the unfortunate events that *did* take place.

Once we finished that list, I asked Marge to do something I've been doing for many years. I asked her if there was anything she could think of right now in her life for which she was *grateful*. She thought for a moment, and said, " I'm grateful for my son." she paused, "I'm grateful for my granddaughter." She paused again, "And I'm grateful for my son's girlfriend. She's a sweetheart, and she's real good for him." Now she was on a roll. "I'm grateful that it didn't rain on my way here. I'm grateful for Muffin even though she costs me a lot of money at the vet." In the next few minutes Marge created a long list.

> River's gratitude list: I'm grateful to you for buying and reading this book. Grateful for Judy, co-conspirator on this book and so many of my life's works, grateful for Tom, co-conspiring on the CD, and all the other music we've created together. Grateful to my mother for allowing me to brush her long, thick hair on Friday evenings when I was a child....

Since this is a book about finding and experiencing love, happiness, and power in your life, I would like you to practice focusing first on what *you* have. That doesn't mean we won't acknowledge the difficulty, pain, and struggle. I just recommend that as part of this journey, you take some time to enjoy what you do have by keeping a gratitude inventory. As you'll see by reading mine, you can be grateful for anything you choose, anything you think of, from any moment of your life. Just start the sentence with *I am grateful for (or to) ....*

> Robert Emmons has conducted research funded by the National Institute of Health on gratitude. His research concludes, among other things, that grateful people reported higher levels of positive emotions and lower levels of depression and stress.

Throughout this journey, I'll be asking you to write things down or practice the exercises I present. You might even want to start a conspiracy journal--your own private account of what's going on for you, how the ideas in the book are affecting you, how you would have said something more effectively, how an idea might be inspiring you to act or change a way of thinking.

While the journey will likely be more deeply textured and more fully experienced if you engage in the activities I suggest, you can do this experience any way you choose. It's your book; it's your moment; it's your life.

I would also like you to do something else for yourself. Too often in our busy, harried lives, we forget how to care for ourselves, and then we forget *to* care for ourselves. I would like you to spend a day this week writing down everything that you do for yourself that gives you pleasure, helps you relax, reduces your stress, makes you feel proud, gives you satisfaction, and so on. It could be workouts, walks, paying some bill that's nagging at you. Listening to that piece of music you love so much. Making a call that was weighing on your mind, reaching out to someone you want to know, or someone you miss, getting that massage or pedicure, whatever "floats your boat."

And remember your gratitude list.

There are only two ways to live your life. One is as though nothing is a miracle. The other is as though everything is a miracle.
Albert Einstein

More Gratitude: I am grateful to Ed for teaching me to read and not really wanting to set me on fire. Grateful for my cousins Marilyn, Jeanie, Meem, Annie, and Faye for educating me about the feminine in the universe. I'm grateful for Jimmy Z., Ronnie B., and Michael G. for their friendship. I'm grateful to Rick for helping me claim my name. I'm grateful for Mary Ann and Carla for bringing their love into our family. I'm grateful to Marlo for bringing her love and her family into my life. I'm grateful to Emma Goldman and Tom Paine for their inspiration. I'm grateful for militant non-violent revolutionaries everywhere. I'm grateful for the word energy of Alice Walker, Marge Piercy, and John Stoltenberg. I'm grateful for rich dark creamy chocolate, fresh strawberries, and ripe bananas.

YOU ASKED FOR IT!

Learning how to get what you want (most of the time)

Some Stories:

Jack, a graduate of one of our batterers groups, told us a story at one of our extended support group meetings.

"For a long time my agreement with my wife was that she was to do the wash and I was supposed to pick up the dog crap in the backyard. Now I've got two, just two shirts I wear for bowling, and for years she always made sure one of them was clean each week. Then a couple months ago, suddenly I went to get my shirt, and it wasn't there. She wasn't home, so I went down to the laundry room, and sure enough, I found both my shirts in the dirty clothes pile. So, I figured what the hell, I'll wear something else tonight. And that was fine. Then about two weeks later, the same thing happened again. It happened again two weeks later. And then she did the same thing this week. I tried to give her a hint last week about being sure she washed everything when she came upstairs with the clothes. She didn't get it, so I figured I'd get the message across to her. So I didn't pick up the crap at all last week, and with four dogs that's a lot of crap. She was playing in the backyard with our niece yesterday, and they both stepped in

a pile. When she came in all bent out of shape, I just said don't talk to me, until you start cleaning up the crap you're supposed to clean up. She got all outraged, and we almost got into a major blow up. I took a time out."

My client, April, told me one day that she felt like punching her little sister. At the time, April was clearly a non-violent, easy going person. Her younger sister was staying at April's place.
"So, what makes you want to punch Denise?"
"She's just so selfish!"
I acknowledged that selfishness can be a problem, and asked how Denise was being selfish.
"She just is. She doesn't think about anybody else's needs."

"Is there anything she's doing in relation to your needs? Anything that's particularly bugging you about her selfishness today?"

"Yes. She won't go out tonight." April proceeded to explain to me that in the three weeks that Denise had been there, April and her partner had not had the opportunity to be alone, and this night was the anniversary of the first time she and Joyce, her partner, had made love.

"I asked Denise if she could find something to do tonight, and she told me she doesn't know

anybody, and doesn't have any place to go. So she'd rather not go out."

Roger lent his friend and long time neighbor some money over a month ago when she was in a bind. She had promised to return it as soon as she got her check. They've seen each other a number of times since then, but she hasn't said a word about the money. Last night he saw her getting a pizza delivery, and he reports feeling hurt and angry since then.

HOW TO INCREASE THE CHANCES OF GETTING WHAT I WANT

OBSERVE THE UNIVERSAL RULE:

It is *MY* job to make it as easy as possible for another person to give me what I want.

Please repeat that statement between three and thirty times: *It is MY job to make it as easy as possible for another person to give me what I want.*

It is MY job...... (maybe you should keep a hand mirror next to you--and look into it as you say it again---)
It is MY job to ..... and again. Whose job is it?

FOUR STEPS TOWARDS SUCCESSFULLY DOING THAT JOB:

1. Get in touch with what I feel.

2. Get clear about what I want from this person in this situation.

3. Make a direct statement of feeling.

4. Ask for what I want.

THE FIRST STEP is particularly hard for most men. We are taught from our earliest years to ignore most of our feelings. Anger is acceptable. Excitement is acceptable, but we have little experience allowing ourselves to stay with our hurt, or fear, or feelings of abandonment, or really gushy elation. Believe me, this training gets in the way of getting what you really want or need. While women struggle less with getting in touch with feelings, it still can be a problem acknowledging them because you are taught that yours are just not that important.

Nevertheless, it's important to know what you're feeling if you're going to get what you actually want. So, once you've clarified for yourself what you feel, you must move to

Feeling words: Happy, confident, frightened, lonely, relieved, surprised, miserable, hurt, ecstatic, envious, pained, frustrated, determined, bored, worried, silly, lost, torn, awkward, adrift, anxious, excited, pleased, comfortable, shaky, disparaged, guilty, elated,....

THE SECOND STEP. There's a simple logic at work here. We can't ask for what we want if we don't know what it is. For instance, you're dependent on a co-worker's input to complete a project today. You wait for her to show up. She comes in an hour late. In step one you get in touch with your feelings (anxiety, frustration, fear…..). Now what do you want from her? Acknowledgement that she was late? An apology? A commitment never to do it again? A commitment to put in extra time to finish the project? Assurance that she will take responsibility if the project doesn't get completed on time? There are lots of possibilities, so you have to decide which you want from her.

THE THIRD STEP is difficult because we are just not used to making direct statements of our feelings. Both men and women feel vulnerable (there's a feeling word) when we put our inner selves out there. Since men are trained against it (*what are you--a little girl?*), it's particularly scary for us.

Nevertheless, research has shown that people are much more receptive to our requests when we have given them a glimpse of our feelings. So what is a direct statement of feelings? *"Sheila, I am very anxious about getting our project done, and I am hurt that you have come in so late, knowing what I might be going through."* This sentence has the two *key* ingredients. The speaker takes ownership of her/his feelings (*I*) and the speaker names feelings: *anxious, hurt.*
How about this one? *"Sheila I feel that you are really inconsiderate and irresponsible for keeping me waiting."* Does that sound direct to you? It might, but it is not direct. Why? Where are the feelings? Inconsiderate is not a feeling. Irresponsible is not a feeling. Besides, the speaker is labeling *Sheila* with these words, not expressing anything about her/him self. The speaker is also

committing a common and serious sin against assertive communications. S/he is using the word *feel* when s/he is actually stating a belief or a judgment. *"I **feel** you're a disgusting, moldy, pompous creep with no consideration for anybody."*

After the listener sets your car on fire, you can't figure out what the problem was.

"I was only expressing my feelings."

As you can see, it's important to not pollute the process. When done properly, expressing your feelings will help you get what you want, not start a fire. I've included an abbreviated quiz, at the end of the chapter, about direct statements of feeling, given to me over thirty years ago by David Pointer. Using what you've read here, see if you can pick out the direct statements.

THE FOURTH STEP is usually the scariest for most of us. It is scarier for many women because you've usually been taught not to directly ask for what you want. This step is really based on a very simple concept. If I want something from you, asking for it is the most efficient way to increase the likelihood I'm going to get it. Picture yourself walking into a fast food restaurant. You would like to be served a soda.

Rather than asking the person behind the cash register for a soda, you stand there. How quickly do you think she or he will figure out what you want and give it to you? Now you can attempt to get the message across indirectly by perhaps licking your lips. You could say something to the person who's just picked up a drink at the counter, loud enough that the employee will hear. *"Boy, I bet that soda tastes really good."* It certainly is possible that over a period of time you could come up with enough indirect actions that the employee, if she or he had the time and patience, would come to understand what you wanted from them. It seems to me, however, that it would be a lot easier and quicker to say directly, *"I'd like a large soda, please."*

I'm sure you see how difficult it would be for the employee to figure out what you want. That employee even has the advantage of working from a limited list of choices (whatever's on the menu) S/he does not even have to consider any of the myriad of options that humans have in normal intercourse with each other. It can often be much more difficult to figure out what your friend/brother/mother/ sister/partner might want in any given situation, without them telling you directly. Unfortunately, we spend a lot of time guessing or assuming because we don't know.

If we look at the story told by group member, Jack, above, and we examine Jack's wife's reported response to his hint *about being sure she washed everything when she came upstairs with the clothes*, we can see the ineffectiveness in action. Indirectness is usually ineffective at helping us get what we want. Even when it works, it is extremely inefficient because of the likelihood of misunderstanding inherent in the process. **Remember**, it is your job…..

So let's review the stories of Jack, April, and Roger with the four steps of getting what you want in mind.

1. Get in touch with what I feel.

2. Get clear about what I want from this person in this situation.

3. Make a direct statement of feeling.

4. Ask for what I want.

Members of the men's support group immediately complimented Jack on his action to take a time out when he was feeling his anger rising. It's his job to do whatever is necessary to make sure he doesn't behave in any way that might intimidate or bully his partner. The group challenged him, however, on his frustrating indirectness and what was identified as passive-aggressive behavior with the dog feces. They told him that they didn't believe that it was simply an indirect way to ask for what he wanted. Rather, he was trying to punish his wife. After some discussion, Jack acknowledged that they were right, and promised to apologize to his wife as soon as possible.

Knowing the four steps, what would you have felt? What would you have wanted from your partner? What would you have done or asked for, if you were Jack? When would you have done it?

April wanted to punch her sister because *"She's just so selfish!"*
So what do you think April was feeling? Was this just about her sister refusing to go tonight? There's actually no way for us or Denise to know, since April hasn't identified what's actually going on with her. What might you feel in the circumstances? Knowing the four steps, what might you want from Denise? What would you have done or asked for, if you were April? When would you have done it?

Roger seems to be in touch with his feelings about his friend and neighbor not paying back what she owes him. Although it's been over a month since he lent her the money, he reports feeling hurt and angry since last night. What would you feel? When would you have started feeling it? Keeping in mind the four steps, what would you have said? What would you have done?

When I present these four steps in workshops or in session to clients I often hear that the participants have *tried* to be assertive, *"but it doesn't work."* When the speaker is questioned closely, it usually turns out that they have not followed these four steps. Certainly, however, there will be times when no matter how assertive we are, we will not get what we want from another person. That's life. We all know the ancient wisdom--

Sometimes the other person may retreat to some behaviors to avoid responding directly to your request, or might have some legitimate issues that block their willingness to positively respond.

You can't always get what you want, but if you try sometime/ you just might find/you get what you need.
Jagger & Richards

Three methods that help us get what we want:
(After we are sure we have openly listened)

A. Circle: No matter where the other speaker takes you, always bring the conversation back around to *"but right now what I would like from you is..."*

B. Acceptance: Sometimes a speaker may bring up something you have done in the past as an indirect rationale for not being willing to accommodate your request. If you believe the essence of what they are saying is true, it's important to acknowledge and accept what they've said, and offer to discuss it further with them, and be willing to schedule a time to do so, *"but right now..."*

C. Acknowledgement: Sometimes a speaker may bring up something they say you have done as an indirect rationale for not accommodating your request. If you believe this to be untrue or if you're uncertain of the facts, you must acknowledge the other person's position, and express a willingness to discuss the matter at another time. Be willing to suggest a specific time to discuss their grievance, *"but right now...."*

Let's look at an example of this process in action.

LeBron lives with his roommate, Kobe. They alternate each week between taking out the garbage and washing the dishes. This has been Kobe's week to wash the dishes, but he has hardly done them, and it's late Thursday afternoon. LeBron has his new special friend coming over tonight.
LeBron: *"Dude, I've got somebody special coming*

in a couple hours and I'm feeling kind of anxious (direct statement of feeling) *that this place is not going to be cleaned up. Would you please take care of the dishes* (asking for what he wants).*"*
Kobe: *"Awh Man, I'm busy right now with this game. Why don't you do 'um?"*
LeBron: *"Well, this is your week, and you've let them pile up. Besides, I'm busy cleaning the other rooms."*
Kobe: *"Look, I'm always cleaning up after you. You haven't taken out the garbage all week, but I'm not giving you a hard time."*
LeBron: *"I'm sorry if you've had to clean up after me, and I'd be happy to talk to you about the garbage another time*(acceptance), *but right now, I'd like you to do what you've agreed to do this week, and get the dishes done before Savannah comes over* (circle).
Kobe: *"Man, you are always getting' into my stuff and interrupting what I'm doin' like my stuff isn't as important as yours."*
LeBron: *"I'm not sure I agree with that, but I'd be happy to talk with you about it* (acknowledgement), *but right now I really need you to take care of those dishes* (circle).
Kobe: *"Yeah right. You're always sayin' you're gunna talk about stuff, but you never do."*
LeBron: *"I'm really sorry you feel that way. I don't know about the past, but I'll tell you right now, I'm willing to talk about anything you need*

to talk about. (acknowledgement) *Let's figure out a time when we're both available to sit down, while you're startin' the dishes* (circle).
Kobe: *"Okay, man, as soon as I finish the game."*

Remember, there will always be some people who just will not be willing to do what you request, but most of us, most of the time, unless we have some unfinished business, will tend to want to oblige someone who is letting us know how they feel and what they want.

Does this sound easy to you?
Difficult?
Impossible?

If it does sound difficult, I can promise you that it will get easier and easier to do as you more frequently do it.

HERE'S ANOTHER RULE

It is your right to say *No*.

WE ALL HAVE THE RIGHT TO SAY *NO*.
That includes you.
Repeat this thirty times today: *I have the right to say No. I have the right to say no. I have the right to say no. I have the right to say no….*
If you are someone who has a problem saying

"No,"

Remember to *<u>give yourself the space</u>* you need to make a decision, even if someone wants an immediate answer from you.

"No."
"No thank you. Not right now."
"No, I'd rather not."
"I'm not sure, *but if you need an answer at this moment, then the answer will have to be no.*"
NO

NO

NO

NO

NO.

While saying *yes* is a wonderful opening to the universe, saying *No*, when it's in your best interest, can really be a lot of fun, too. *FUN!?* Riding a bicycle is fun for most of us, but it was also quite difficult for most of us to get used to doing it. Many of us would not call falling down and skinning our elbows and knees fun while we learned the *riding--a--bike* skill. This is just as true as we trip or stumble practicing the *saying--No* skill; however, with practice, you'll be having fun, and contributing to a profound revolution.

*To hold the word **no** in my mouth like a gold coin, something valued, something possible. To teach the **no** to our daughters. To value their **no** more than their compliant yes. To celebrate **no**. To hold the word **no** in your fist and refuse to give it up. To support the woman who says, **no, no, no. I will not.** To love the **no**. To cherish the **no**, which is so often our first word. No--the means to transformation.*
Louise Edrich

While **YES** is most certainly the answer to the question of life, the yes means nothing if we don't experience the *power* to say

NO

I've included a partial list of rights here. After you read it, see how many you can add. Just keep in mind the caveat, "But I do not have the right to intimidate, manipulate, emotionally, physically, or sexually abuse another person." As long as the rights you list don't do that, they can only help you and those around you to respect both you and themselves.

BECAUSE I AM ALIVE, I HAVE THE RIGHT TO:

Ask for what I want.
Have my needs be as important as the needs of others.
Take pride in my age and experience.
Be myself.
Say I don't know.
Feel and express anger.
Be believed.

But I do not have the right to intimidate, manipulate, emotionally, physically, or sexually abuse another person.

Make mistakes.
Have my opinions given respect.
Offer no justification for my actions or opinions..
Grow and learn.
Have privacy and personal space.
Say I don't understand.
Say *No*

But I do not have the right to intimidate, manipulate, emotionally, physically, or sexually abuse another person.

Tell someone my needs.
Make illogical decisions.
Judge my own behavior, feelings, and thoughts.
Change my mind.
Say I don't agree.
Be proud of my accomplishments.
Trust my feelings, perceptions, judgments, and intuition.
And…..

But I do not have the right to intimidate, manipulate, emotionally, physically, or sexually abuse another person.

CHALLENGES

So, let's say you've practiced the assertiveness techniques over and over, yet when you need to use them you don't. I suppose if I knew how to read a compass or use a GPS device but never left my house, my GPS and compass reading skills wouldn't be very useful to me. I also might be quite rusty and somewhat unfamiliar with the most useful ways to utilize these tools, if I didn't often use them. It is the same situation with our assertiveness skills if we don't allow ourselves the opportunity to use *them*.

Like so much we're told, it's a lot easier *said* than done. Numerous clients, students, workshop participants, and friends have explained to me that if they don't like themselves, if they're afraid of conflict, if they think their feelings are not important enough, if they don't want to create complications for another, it doesn't matter how well they know the assertiveness steps, they're not going to use them.

Many of us operate out of what's known as a codependent position. Before we react to someone's behavior, we have to examine their motives. The idea seems to be, if I can understand why someone is jumping up and down on my toe, I can tolerate the pain. While in some very specific circumstances this might be of some value, overwhelmingly, our lives will be much more satisfying and fulfilling if we simply stay focused on what our own needs and desires are, and commit to communicating those to the other person.

"I don't know why you're jumping up and down on my toe, but it hurts. Please stop it."
"But you don't understand!"
"Maybe not, but you're hurting my toe, and I'm leaving if you don't stop immediately."

There's nothing inherently counter-productive in being willing to discuss the other person's motives **AFTER** they have stopped doing the thing that hurts you.

> *Recognize that being assertive is not the same as being aggressive. Assertiveness is insisting that you be heard; aggressiveness is insisting that you get your way. Not everyone should get their way, but everyone-- including you-- should be heard.*
> Sam Deep & Lyle Sussman

Sometimes it's easier for us to get this when we are thinking of another's wellbeing. If you see your young child is hitting the dog with a stick, you don't inquire about their motives; you act. After you've prevented further harm, you may choose to enter into a conversation. Remember to do the same for yourself as you would do for your cousin, the dog.

Any and all of us may have issues that keep us from fully using these skills such as:

1. We're not used to communicating our needs or desires directly.
2. We're afraid to create a headache for the other person.
3. We're afraid of a possible conflict
4. We're too overwhelmed; we just can't handle facing anything else.
5. We don't believe our needs or desires are important enough.
6. We don't believe we deserve to get what we want.
7. We believe we're destined to be hurt or disappointed.

The first of these challenges can be met by simply acting. The more we practice a new skill, the more natural it becomes.

The rest of these barriers will be addressed as we continue this journey.

A Final Note

Based on the work of Sam Deep and Lyle Sussman I suggest a few more things to consider:

1. When you feel wronged, name it right away. Delaying it only causes the eventual conversation

to be more difficult.

2. Realize that when you don't name your feelings, you are contributing to the destruction of the relationship.
Sublimated feelings don't disappear. You'll begin acting negatively toward this person for reasons that neither of you will readily understand.

3. Never assume someone is trying to hurt you when their actions can be explained by incompetence--give them credit for being stupid or insensitive. By being assertive, you may help them identify behavior they might be quite willing to change.

4. If you get a bad reaction to asserting yourself, analyze the experience. Learn from the result, and decide if you could do a better job next time.
Don't take the experience as proof that you should never assert yourself with anyone again.

Direct Statement of Feelings Quiz
(D=Direct. I=Indirect)

1. Shut Up! Not another word out of you!
2. I'm beginning to resent your interruptions.
3. You're a wonderful person.
4. I feel you are a wonderful person.
5. You didn't come to see me in the hospital.
6. I'm discouraged.
7. I feel this job is miserable.
8. I feel alone and isolated in my group.
9. We all like this quiz.
10. I am frustrated by this weird quiz.

Answers: 1-I, 2-D, 3-I, 4-I, 5-I, 6-D, 7-I, 8-D, 9-I, 10-D.

More Gratitude: I'm grateful to Omar Vizquel, Robbie Alomar, and Kenny Lofton for their ballet on the field. I'm grateful to Victor for friendship and for helping me spark. I'm grateful to Amos, my colleague of almost twenty years in the quest to help men become allies to women. Grateful to Bud Stern for guidance. To my clients for their trust, for the men who committed to the groups, for all the women who have tolerated and taught me. I'm grateful to the healers who grace the planet with their spirit and their love. I'm grateful for Lake Erie (into which I regularly flow), for stevia, flax seeds, and any plants I can enjoyably eat. I'm grateful for Jackie Wilson, Buddy Ebsen, Eleanor Powell, the Nicholas Brothers, Fred Astaire, and my dad for their moves.

I

CAN'T

FIND

MYSELF

The stories we tell ourselves, particularly the silent or barely audible ones, are very powerful. One must open the window to see them, the door to possibility.
Susan Griffin

We become what we behold.
Marshall McLuhan

Probably the most important journey we will ever take is the journey inward. Unless we know who we are, how can we possibly offer what we have? I need to know my story…all of it.
Anne Wilson Schaef

We are 'we' before we are 'I'. John Bradshaw

"I can't find myself." "I've got to find myself."
"PLEASE! Help me find my self."

These words were often heard and repeated throughout the 1970's. They were commonly represented as examples of a sense of self absorption by members of the so-called *Me Generation*. And they became the object of ridicule and jokes in the media. However humorous they may seem, the basic concept they expressed is a very important one for moving towards happiness, joy, and love in our lives. None of us can go anywhere without bringing our *self* along.

In the 1940s and 50s the concept of "self" became associated with two respected researchers, Carl Rogers and Abraham Maslow. Carl Rogers posited that each of us is born with an *organismic self*, but that we lose track of that self as our *self concept* is created. That self concept is developed through the environment in which we grow. So, the adults and others in our life teach us, in part, who we are. The natural self, in tune with the universe, is partially or totally lost to us if those around us do not act with unconditional positive regard for us-- showing us through their actions that we are intrinsically okay. If that doesn't happen, then we

> *Too many of us seem to be searching for something "out there" to make our lives complete. We feel alienated, lonely and empty. No matter what we do or have, we never feel fulfilled.*
> Susan Jeffers

grow up being out of touch with our "self" or living with this dis-ease because of the incongruence created by the contrast between who we feel we are deep inside and who we've been taught we are. So, yes, to have a chance at happiness, according to Rogers, we need to either *find* our self, or come to some kind of satisfying peace with that inner organismic self.

Abraham Maslow developed the notion of a hierarchy of needs. He argued that there were levels of needs that must be satisfied before we could move on to the next level of needs, eventually getting to the levels of an *actualized self* and a *transcendent self,* which is where he suggested we could find happiness. The lower levels were involved in pursuing what he termed *deficiency needs*. The upper levels are called *growth needs*.

The four lower levels are:
1) *Physiological: hunger, thirst, basic physical comforts, etc.*
2) *Safety/security: not having to experience danger.*
3) *Belongingness and Love: affiliate with others, be accepted.*
4) *Esteem: to achieve, be competent, gain approval and recognition.*

Level 1. The argument goes that before we can focus on anything else, we first must be fed and be free from thirst, be sheltered, and have the other basic physical needs met.

When I was a teenaged poet lecturing my mother and father on how empty their working class lives were, my mother had a constant refrain that served as a defense of her life and a caution for mine. *"If it's so good, put the money on the table."*

If it's so good, put the money on the table. To my mother, whose family had lived in a tent in a municipal park for months during the great depression, who with her brother, stole apples from the fruit stand so her family could eat, it was very clear that if you couldn't pay your way in the society, nothing else could matter.

Level 2. So if we have enough to eat and a place to stay, we also must then be able to feel safe. If we're witnessing violence or are the target of it, it is hard to focus on much else.

My client, Ray, described what it was like after school at home. *We, my older brother and me, played in the dining room, on the floor with our trucks or our soldiers while my mother made dinner. The radio or the TV was usually on. I remember laughing and rough housing,*

> *In West Africa there is a belief that to be harsh with a child is to cause the soul to retreat from the body. Liberating our bodies from images and actions bent on destroying the soul means determining for ourselves a definition of life free from internalized misogyny and inferiority.*
> K. Louise Schmidt

but always listening. And then finally it would come. I could hear his car door slam and my stomach would turn. I could hardly breathe. Ricky's eyes would get big. We would grab everything and scramble up the stairs, into our room. Sometimes I'd go right to the closet and get on the floor, bury myself in the dirty clothes. I didn't care. I didn't want to be hurt again. And I knew I couldn't stop him."

Some things a child might like to hear: *Super job, marvelous, terrific, that's incredible! How nice. Beautiful! Remarkable bravo! I knew you could do it! Outstanding! You are really something,, Well done. I trust you. You brighten my day. You're a treasure. Awesome! You're so kind! What an imagination! You're precious. You're important. I love you. You're a hard worker. Great work. You'll get it. Thank you. Please.*

Maria, a student at the alternative high school where I worked many years ago, told me how she used to get in trouble at her elementary school for not having her hair brushed, or having her hands and face washed. She couldn't explain to her earlier teachers, but she explained to me that her mother sat at a table in the kitchen every morning, and Maria had to pass that table on her way to the bathroom to get ready for school. Most mornings her mother was either still drunk or severely hung over. Most mornings as Maria attempted to pass her, her mother would reach out and grab her by the hair, and pull her to the floor and scream at her for some real or imagined trespass. Sometimes she would beat her with a brush. Maria eventually cut all her hair off so it would be more difficult for

her mother to grab her.
Ray and Maria would both have a hard time focusing on much besides their fear each day, so it certainly would be difficult for them to focus on the next level.

Level 3. Human beings have been called herd animals in terms of affiliation needs. To be okay, most of us must feel connected to a small band of others. In our culture this is usually family, friends, small social groupings. The important issue is that we feel accepted by those around us.

Other things children might like:
A big smile.
A big hug.
A big kiss.

John grew up in a home with a mom who was 43 and dad who was 60 when John was born. They were both immigrants from Eastern Europe. They didn't trust their neighbors, and wouldn't allow John to have a friend in the neighborhood or at school. He was not allowed to go inside anyone's house, and no one was allowed in his home. There was almost no talking in the home, no expression of emotion. If he committed even the most minor infraction, there would be severe corporal punishment by either parent. They had to approve any book or magazine that John brought into the home. He was never allowed to close the door to his room. No modern music could be played in the home. As a teenager, John had a 9pm curfew through high school.

"That didn't much matter," John explained to me, *"Since I was too afraid to talk to anyone, and when someone talked to me I never knew how to act."*

Predictably, John found himself unable to form affiliations with any peers. was unable to feel connected. He never experienced the sense of belonging with others. So would it be any wonder that John could not move to the next level on the hierarchy?

Level 4. FINALLY, to move to the upper levels of Maslow's hierarchy we must first believe that we are competent in some way that is valued by our group. We must feel like we are able to accomplish things that we believe are necessary. It is only then that we can allow ourselves to focus on our growth needs.

What did you hear from your caregivers? What do you wish you heard? What have you said to your children?

Laura, who probably suffered from some form of Attention Deficit Disorder, was told by parents, teachers, and early friends, because her attention span was so short, that she was "dumb." Her mother and her teachers constantly criticized her work, and she eventually dropped out of high school. She got a job at a donut shop, but after messing up the coffeemaker a number of times, was fired, and spent years moving from one dead end job to another. Laura never felt competent or accepted for her accomplishments. It was extremely unlikely that Laura would move on to the upper levels of Maslow's hierarchy.

Each of the folks I mentioned here were inhibited from moving from one or another of the so called lower levels of Maslow's hierarchy, and though each, with varying success, found ways to survive, cope, and sometimes thrive, all of them had trouble asserting themselves with others. All had trouble allowing themselves to ask for what they wanted from others. All struggled to become self-actualized or happy.

> *I believe what all of us are really searching for is this divine essence within ourselves.*
> Susan Jeffers

SO, WHAT is *self-actualization*? It has been described as the stage when one seeks edifying information for growth, when one feels basically content with oneself, when one feels free to reach for further connection. As one feels the former, s/he develops *self-transcendence,* a profound sense of connection with all things and all beings. According to Maslow, it is in this stage that we experience wisdom.

Many theorists have enlarged and expanded on the work of Rogers and Maslow as they have explored the issues of happiness, joy, and love. Let's continue on this path.

*Like so much of life, it begins with Active Listening: compassionate, open hearted, open minded listening. Just sit in their (children's) presence. We **must** be on their side.* Nancy Carlson Paige

HOW

DO

I

GET

TO

HAPPYLAND?

Live as if you liked yourself and it might happen: reach out, keep reaching out, keep bringing in.... Marge Piercy

I find ecstasy in living; the mere essence of living is joy enough. Emily Dickinson

So, where is *Happyland*? What's it mean to be happy? What is happiness anyway? It is hard to find something if we don't know what we're looking for. What do you picture in your mind when you hear the word, *happiness*? What is the difference between happiness and joy?

It won't go in words/ but I know that it's real.
Willie Nelson

Common dictionary definitions of happiness usually include: feeling pleasure, contentment or *joy*; satisfaction.

Common dictionary definitions of joy include: feelings of great *happiness* or pleasure, *especially of an elevated or spiritual kind.*

While there seems to be some overlap, for our purposes, it is the above definition of *joy* that we'll be working toward here. So if we're seeking this joyful happiness, what's it made of? What are the ingredients, and how do we get them? What's so great about being happy?

According to Professor Sonja Lyubomirsky of The University of California, happy people tend to get sick less, have better immune systems, and live longer than others. Happy people are rated by those around them as more socially adept, more competent, and even more likely to get to heaven than their peers.

Rogers would argue that integrating your organismic self with your self concept would produce happiness. Maslow would say that the wisdom produced by reaching the self transcendence level would produce happiness.

What are five words you associate with happiness?

Tom Stevens predicts that certain values themes/beliefs are fundamental to what he calls harmonious functioning. These include values like maximizing happiness and love for all, empathy, understanding, forgiveness, truth, knowledge, learning, control, self-discipline, self development, integrity, optimistic belief in positive forces controlling the universe, no expectations about what the person is owed by life, gratitude for all that they have, healthy activity and play, and beauty.
Wow! That's quite a list.

Ryan Howell of San Francisco University conducted a study that seems to conclude that new experiences create happiness. His study of 154 people ages 19 to 50 showed that buying *experiences*--such as vacations, going to the theater or renting a sailboat, gave people more happiness than buying material things. "People report a sense of feeling invigorated or inspired."

Gallup recently did a survey involving over

350,000 people, attempting to measure well-being. Examples of the questions include: Did you smile or laugh a lot yesterday? Are you satisfied or dissatisfied with your job or the work you do? Did you eat healthy all day yesterday? Do you feel safe walking alone at night in the city or area where you live?

The survey examines individual eating and exercise habits, work environment, and access to basic necessities, among other criteria.

Eric Nielson, a spokesperson for Gallup said, "It's not just about physical health. It's about their ability to contribute at work and be more productive, and it's about feeling engaged in a community and wanting to improve that community."

Probably due to the sense of choice and opportunity, people with higher incomes tended to score higher on the index.
Gallup plans to continue this "wellbeing index" survey for the next twenty-five years.

Iyanla Vansant might argue that the following will contribute to happiness:
1. Begin within, take quiet time alone.
2. Trust your head, follow your first thought.
3. Don't be fooled by appearances.

4. Plan prayerfully; prepare purposefully; proceed positively; pursue persistently.
5. Be willing to be wrong.
6. Be flexible.
7. Do the best you can where you are with what you have.
8. Be prepared.
9. See the invisible; feel the intangible; achieve the impossible.
10. Focus+Courage+Willingness to Work=Miracles
11. Help somebody else.
12. When in doubt, *pray.*

Don Miguel Ruiz might posit that using the four agreements will up our chances for happiness:

1. Be impeccable with your word - Speak with integrity. Say only what you mean. Avoid using the word to speak against yourself or others. Use the power of your word for truth and love.

2. Don't take anything personally - Nothing others do is because of you. What others say and do is a projection of their own reality, their own understanding of the world. When you are immune to the opinions and actions of others, you will not needlessly suffer.

3. Don't make assumptions - Find the courage to ask questions and to express what you really want.

Communicate with others as clearly as you can to avoid misunderstandings. This agreement alone can completely transform your life.

4. Always do your best - Your best is going to change from moment to moment; it will be different when you are healthy or sick. Simply do the best you can in the moment, and you will avoid self-judgment, self-abuse, and regret.

Gary McClain & Eve Adamson, in their book, <u>Empowering your life with joy</u>, write:

The possibility to manifest joy is there in every moment, every situation, every breath of life-- whether the conditions seem conducive to joy or not. Whether you feel up to the "work" of creating joy, or not, it is there, waiting. Inherent. Yours.

Joy is finding beauty in ugliness while still recognizing the ugliness. Joy is acknowledging both pain and the growth it inspires. Joy is courageous and won't be thwarted. Joy is empathetic, sometimes cheerful and sometimes quietly serene, but joy always recognizes humanity and the common bond we all share. It is the soul's rescue crew. It is the spark of the human spirit.

Frances Moore Lappé and Jeff Perkins would argue that curiosity and courage are critical to joyful happiness.

I have compiled a list of common attributes that I and other researchers and clinicians have observed in people who identify themselves as happy:

One Map to Happyland

1. They are Curious. They are frequently asking the next question, wanting to know more about whatever they are facing. They listen.
2. They are Generous. They enjoy giving to others.
3. They are Flexible They are comfortable with the unexpected, confident that they will adjust.
4. They tend to have at least one or two intimate friends/lovers.
5. They are playful and have a self-effacing sense of humor. They are humble. They listen.
6. They do what they consider productive work.
7. They are "problem" centered, rather than ego centered.* They listen.
8. They live life as though there is usually abundance, accept the limits of their power, and don't worry a lot about what they don't or won't have. They listen.
9. They have a clear set of guiding principles by which they work to live.
10. They experience hope easily.
11. They are accountable for their actions.
12. They tend to believe they are connected to something larger than themselves.

*A person is problem-centered when they are able to stay focused on whatever the challenge is that they confront. They are not sidetracked by how they will be perceived or by fear of failure.

Happiness is found along the way, not at the end of the road. Seen on a roadside sign.

The day you let go of your dreams is the day you let go of your life. Lil Rounds (An *American Idol* contestant)

Yeah, life hurts like hell, but this is how I keep going. I have a sense of humor, I've got my brothers and sisters. I've got the ability to make something out of nothing. I can clap my hands and make magic. Bill Jones

As Eric Copage writes in his book, <u>Black Pearls,</u> we each need to find a way to clap our hands and make magic. As he says, we all have burdens, disappointments, and sorrows, but if we focus on those experiences, it is hard to find joy.

Joy comes for Bill Jones from his dancing, his friends, and his sense of humor. Where does your joy come from?

Think of five things you need to be happy today.

McClain and Adamson offer this meditation as a Joy-Full Exercise. Take some, full, slow, deep breaths and repeat:
My feelings come and go. I can watch them come. I can feel them, and I can let them go. They are not me.

And

Remember to laugh a lot. A lot.

We know from both our experiences and the researchers, laughing can make us feel better. We don't know exactly why, but we know it does.

Against the assault of laughter, nothing can stand.
Mark Twain

We do know that when you laugh, three parts of your brain light up. An intellectual part processing the information, an emotional area that produces the giddy feeling, and a movement area that causes your facial muscles to move.

According to John Morreall, at The College of William & Mary, laughter is often a playful response to incongruities-stories that don't follow one's expectations. Researchers have also concluded that laughter is a signal to others that a given action is meant "in fun."

So, you want to be happy?

Laugh your socks off!!

"I'd like a quart of love and

two packs of affection,

please."

If I can't love Hitler, I can't love at all. AJ Muste

Love is still the answer--even when I forget what the question is.

MOTHER LOVE

Practicing the art of loving is one way we sustain contact with our "higher self." bell hooks

This is a term commonly used to describe nurturing love. We use the word *mother* interchanged with *nurture* because in most of the major cultures on the earth women/mothers are the primary nurturers of children. It is clear, however, that many women do not feel comfortable in that role, and many men do.

So what is this *mother* love? Geneen told me she would spend hours lying on her mother's bed while her mother was at work in the evenings. She just loved the sweet scent of her mother's hair and skin. She could close her eyes and see her mother's smile. Feel her skin against hers. Many of my clients talk about their grandmother's hugs, or how safe they felt being held.

Somewhere on almost any gratitude list I make will be my thanks for early touch I received from my mother, father, and grandfather. I close my eyes and feel myself held in my father's powerful hands and arms. I feel my grandfather's and my mother's tender touch, and I feel warm and safe. *Mother* Love.

Acceptance, warm regard, tenderness, and affectionate touch: *Mother* Love. Most of us are fortunate enough to receive *some* level of this. Unfortunately, since the challenges to happiness get passed down from generation to generation in a patriarchal/dominator culture like ours, our parents are going to pass down at least some of the dysfunction that's been passed to them. Their nurturing love is going to be at least imperfect, and for some, barely present at all. So, it is unlikely that anyone gets out of childhood without some damage to our understanding of love. Jim, one of the guys in our group has described his interaction with his mother.

She's always treated me good. Always made sure we had enough to eat. Taught me to be responsible. Showed me how to ride my bike, how to tie my shoes, but we're not a touching family. I mean we don't do all that touchy feely stuff in our house. I know my mom loves me. She calls me everyday. Worries about me even though I've been out of the house for ten years. But no, I don't remember, I mean I remember her giving me a peck on the cheek a couple of times, but I can't remember if we ever have hugged. No. I don't think we ever did that.

So here's a mom who apparently cares deeply for her son, yet something in her past has prevented her from giving Jim the touch he so desperately longs for. Well, what's the big deal? How important is touch anyway?

Research tells us that touch is ***crucial*** to emotional, mental, and physical development in mammals. Touch is the first fundamental connection for us as babies. Many studies have shown that babies who do not get enough touch are developmentally impaired. Premature infants gain weight much more quickly if their back and legs are regularly stroked.

Studies have shown that something happens inside us when we are simply gently touched in daily interactions, such as by a store clerk when s/he gives us back our change. When interviewed afterward, we are much more likely to say we had a pleasant experience than if we haven't been touched.

In an experiment many years ago, coins were left in a public phone booth. Immediately after the next person used the phone, the study participant would approach and ask if the person had found any money. Unfortunately, only a little over half the subjects admitted to finding the money. If the same question was asked while the study participant was reaching out, palm up, touching the subject's elbow, the positive response went up by at least twenty percent.

I still remember Phyllis Stoller, a humanities consultant at the alternative school where I was working in the late 1970s. As alternative and creative as our structure and curriculum were, there was something that Phyllis showed us we were missing.

Touch! Loving, nurturing touch. Staff, students, parents were all taught to challenge our attitudes about physical interaction. Phyllis helped us implement a pattern of comfort with physical contact. At first, planned trust and touching exercises were built into academic activities. Then formal group hugs were instituted at our community meetings. Within months, spontaneous group hugs became so common that they started occurring any time three or more community members might be together. We even developed regular group massages that some student groups continued well past graduation.

Why did members of all ages of our Cleveland Urban Learning Community take so enthusiastically to Phyllis's encouragement? Because most of us longed for that nurturing touch.   MOTHER LOVE.

Nurturing touch, however, will only be confusing

for a child if we're not also *consistently* sending the kinds of messages listed in the *I Can't Find Myself* chapter.

There are many forms of love, and there are many ways researchers, poets, songwriters, philosophers, and the rest of us have tried to define it for ourselves.

Eric Fromm wrote about the many different kinds of love in his groundbreaking book, *The Art of Loving*, over fifty years ago. He talked about the love of "God," the love between parent and child, between siblings, the love between friends, and the love between romantic partners.

With the exception of the love of "God," I would contend that all forms of love have mostly the same ingredients.

While the issue of *LOVE* is much bigger than romantic love, so often when we enter a discussion about *love*, we are thinking about *romantic* love. So, let us spend a few pages focusing on this fascinating topic.

I've heard that songbirds take 43 days to

Until we really believe we deserve to be loved, chances are we will not draw healthy love to us. Maybe as a child, we were told we were bad; or maybe we assumed we were unacceptable from the treatment we received.... children feel everything that happens to them, or even around them, is their fault. As adults we rationally know that we were not unlovable as children, and that our parents and other important adults did the best they could considering their own hurts. But knowing we are lovable needs to register in our hearts as well as our minds.
Sue Patton Thoele

> *The Lakota... believe that love is the first wisdom given to us and that all things are derived from that knowledge.*
> Leo Busgaglia

go south in the winter for food, but make the return trip for mating purposes in about 13 days. What's up? Sex?   Love?

Eric Fromm wrote that there were three common misconceptions about romantic love:

1. We confuse falling with being. In my introductory psychology classes I used to tell students, *"I love falling in love. I like to do it thirty--forty times a week."* Of course I was being a little facetious, but I was making one of Fromm's points. That feeling of heady exhilaration, that explosion of sensations throughout our bodies when our chemicals go crazy and our mind can't stop thinking about someone--Guess what? That's not love. That doesn't mean it's not something pretty special. It's what Fromm called *falling in love*, and what many researchers since have called *infatuation* or what Dorothy Tennov has called *limerence.* It is a wonderful chemical process that can intensify our experience of the world. It can be a glorious high, or a terrible, deep anguishing heart wound--but it is *not* love.

Infatuation *can* lead to love. However, it is much more likely that it will not. For, even though most of us don't have the above experience often, it is far more common than the experience of *being in love*. That takes work, time, risk, vulnerability, and a lot more.

2. We confuse being lovable with being loving. When I was much younger, whenever I was around someone I regarded as a potential lover, I would so want to impress them with my knowledge, with my wisdom, with my general "coolness." I was trying to be lovable in one of the ways I knew how. I would talk and talk, and though I asked them their opinions, these folks would pretty much not express much. Of course, I thought they all agreed with everything I said on almost every subject.

Finally, one day I overheard a lover expressing an opinion to someone else, that was totally in opposition to what I thought we both believed. At first I was angry. This person had misrepresented herself to me. Then I started looking at my own behavior.

When we're infatuated with another person, two things happen. Our judgments about the other person go into a kind of suspended animation. We unconsciously work to avoid facing anything about the other person we might not like. We also tend to do everything we can to show them that we are worthy of their love and affection. The clothes we wear, the colognes, oils, and perfumes we apply, the words we use, the attitudes we express, the actions we take, can all be susceptible to this pattern. We are focused on being *lovable*.

Fromm argues that as long as we focus in this way, we can never feel truly loved by the other person, because deep within us we know we are not allowing the person to know who we really are. Therefore, we end up with, *If s/he really knew me, s/he would....* Also, because we are focused on manipulating the other person into cherishing us, we are not focused on actually loving *them*.

3. We confuse process or ability with commodity. As Fromm and many other theorists have contended, *love* is not a commodity that can be purchased. We can purchase gratitude or appreciation with certain actions, but, as Lennon and McCartney told us, *Can't buy me love.* I tried to get a quart at the market yesterday, and they told me they don't stock it. I went on EBay and couldn't find it. No luck on Craig's list. I could find lots of sex, but no love. As Leo Busgaglia has brilliantly posited:

Love is a choice. Capacity to love is not the same as having the *ability* to love. ...it needs to be evoked, studied, taught, and practiced if it is to have any real meaning.

It can be argued that everyone has the *capacity*,

but we need to develop the *ability* to love.
Are you in love? Have you ever been in love? How many times? When you look back now, are there times you thought you were in love when you really weren't? Can there be romantic love that's bad for you?

> Write down five words you associate with love.

In his Triangular Theory of Romantic Love, Robert J. Sternberg argues that there are three components that make up romantic love: Intimacy, Passion, and Commitment.

Many theorists, myself included, believe that, while passion can come out of infatuation, and therefore, lead to intimacy and commitment, sustained passion actually arises from intimacy. We also believe that commitment is a given in all relationships. It actually is present in any conscious actions we take. We make a thousand commitments to ourselves and others each day. Most of them are so common that we take them for granted. We don't direct our attention to them. You put on your turn signal while driving, you're making a commitment to turn. You stand on the curb at the crosswalk while traffic passes, you're committing to not step in the path of a car, etc.

Some would argue that the difference between a loving, close, platonic friendship, and a romantic relationship is the presence or absence of passion. Others suggest that passion exists in both. (Aren't you ever really excited about getting together with your best friend?) It's just that passion in the friendship doesn't include sensual and sexual aspects.

What's important here is that both contain *intimacy*.

Ingredients of Sternberg's Intimacy Component:

1. Desire to promote the welfare of a loved one.
2 Experiencing happiness with the loved one.
3. Having high regard for the loved one.
4. Being able to count on the loved one in times of need.
5. Mutual understanding with the loved one.
6. Sharing one's self and one's possessions with the loved one.
7. Receiving emotional support from the loved one.
8. Giving emotional support to the loved one.
9. Having intimate communication with the loved one.
10 Valuing the loved one in one's life.

What's included in your intimacy list? Is there anything you would add to Sternberg's list?

So, what is Intimacy?
It's common in our society to equate sexuality

with intimacy, when in fact, sexuality is often used to avoid intimacy. So what *is* intimacy? One common definition is that it's a detailed knowledge resulting from a close or long association or study. We gain an *intimate* knowledge of another through long association or study. Have you noticed who's been studying you lately?

I have argued that the most important item on Sternberg's list is number nine. *Having intimate communication with the loved one.* Without that, the rest cannot come. But what then is *intimate* communication? I will explain my interpretation in a few pages.

I have to learn to stop breathing for others.
Mary Smyth

Stanton Peele, a researcher on both love and addiction, lists the following contrasts between the two.
1. Rather than love as an absorption in and by another, love should be an awakening, expansive experience that opens the individual to opportunities within and outside the person not previously available.
2. Rather than love as an idealizing of another, love can be a helping relationship that recognizes the limitations of the other person. Doesn't loving a person mean that we want them to be all *they* can be?
3. Rather than love as something to satiate one's internal hunger, the love assumes mutual value of

each partner, each being worthy of admiration and love.

4. Rather than love as something painful or as a refuge from a painful world, love can be an intensification of the pleasure and an inspiration in life.

5. Rather than love as something that incapacitates, it can enhance a person's abilities.

6. Rather than love as an accidental or volatile experience, it can be a natural outgrowth of life.

7. Rather than something immeasurable, it can be measured like friendship and affection.

8. Rather than love as an uncontrollable urge, love can be a heightened state of awareness and responsibility.

The implication of what Peele has stated is that the same addictive drives for drugs or alcohol or other obsessions, are often identified as romantic love, and, in fact, give real *romantic love* a bad name.

Our fears infect our love.
Mary Smyth

There is No Unhealthy Love.
There is no such thing.

Based on Peele's descriptions, do you believe you have been in love? Or have you been in addiction?

Nathaniel Brandon writes about the characteristics he has found in his studies that seem to be consistent in successful romantic relationships. He lists the following about partners:

1. They tend to express love verbally.
2. They tend to be physically affectionate.
3. They tend to express their love sexually.
4. They often express their appreciation and admiration for each other.
5. They participate in mutual self-disclosure.
6. They offer each other an emotional support system.
7. They express love materially with little and large gifts.
8. They operate with benevolence and grace, accepting demands and shortcomings.
9. They create time to be alone together.

Tom G. Stevens, based on studies, suggests nine attributes of a successful romantic relationship.

1. **Democratic, assertive communication and conflict resolution.** Partners seek win-win solutions to conflicts, with clear, caring, understanding, non-defensive, calm, persistent, honest, friendly, non-threatening behaviors.
2. **Open, Honest Communication and Goal Harmony.** They reveal most private and sensitive thoughts and feelings regularly, have shared goals, and feelings of relationship commitment.

3. **Close, Romantic Interactions.** There is romantic attraction, playful, romantic surprises; partners fantasize about each other, go to romantic places, have special celebrations together.
4. **Liberated Roles.** There is equality in decisions, roles, chores/tasks, career priority, some non-stereotypical role behaviors.
5. **Valuing One's Partner--Love and Respect for One's Partner.** Each love, respect, cheerfully do favors for, praise more than criticize partner. Feel free when their partner is home, feel committed not trapped.
6. **Relationship Independence-Autonomy.** Autonomy within committed relationship. Partners feel encouraged and free to pursue own interests and friendships. Each enjoy being alone, having partially separate funds, and believing they could be happy with another person if necessary. They value individual happiness over marriage *per se*.
7. **Positive, Supportive Communication.** Supportive of partner even during disagreements, rarely use negative labels, exaggerations, threats, anger. If one partner gets angry, other usually uses deescalating response.
8. **Collaborative, Non-Manipulative Relationship.** Partners don't act manipulative or controlling. Each feels safe revealing weaknesses. They work together or teach each other effectively.
9. **Separateness.** Spending weekends alone is OK. They don't consult for small decisions.

As you can see, there are consistent themes in all these authors' research conclusions. Healthy romantic love has some very important ingredients. If most of those ingredients aren't present, then we must face that we are not really *in* love.

So what allows us to love our friends, our romantic partners, our family members, the world in general? Where does this love come from, and how do we pass it on?

The mind creates the abyss and the heart crosses over it. Love is the bridge.
Steven Levine

River's Theory of Liberating (Soulful) Love:
I tell you I am serious /in this heart attack,
What we find in each other/ is not something that we lack,
But rather just a little more /of what we each possess/
Even, even, in our separateness./ We are not alone.

Here is the eternal riddle:
Love helps heal us, but without healing, it is difficult to experience love.
Healing helps us experience love, but without love, it is difficult to feel healing.

We will walk through the heart of this conundrum as we continue on this foraging journey.

Whether we speak of romantic love, companion love, familial love, or something more comprehensive, **Here's the secret:** we don't find love by **seeking** it; we find love by **giving** it.

BUT *how can we give it if we don't have it?*

There are a few of us who have grown up in an extraordinarily loving and functional family that helped us keep our developing self-concept in tune, in rhythm, with our organismic self. These folks have felt love from earliest memories, have always been in touch with it, and believe they have plenty to give. For the rest of us, it takes effort that can be very difficult at first because it requires us to trust the unfamiliar. We have to practice accepting ourselves for who we are in this moment. We have to challenge the voice that tells us we must be put down for the smallest infraction, insulted for small mistakes.
What a jerk! I should know that. I am such a screw up! I'll never get this right. Nobody will ever want me. I am such a loser! I can't learn anything. What an idiot! I'll never figure that out. I am so lazy. Why can't I do anything right! What the ---- is wrong with me!

Somewhere there must be a universal list that

unhappy humans have developed and passed on through the millennia with thousands of these lines, in almost every language spoken on the planet. **If you want love in your life**, you are going to have to challenge these mean spirited words that have been deposited in your head.

You are going to have to accept the revolutionary notion that there is nothing wrong with you. What?
There is nothing wrong with you. Oh, you may not be particularly adept at this task or that. You are certainly going to make mistakes. Be socially or physically clumsy. There are some things that are difficult for you to learn. (My list includes trigonometry, cell phones, how not to sing off key, and a few hundred more items.) Your hair's not always going to look the way you would like it. Your body is going to **seem** unacceptable to you. You are going to hurt others at times. You are going to be rejected by others at times. You are going to feel alone and lonely. Not worthy.
BUT----

Guess what? You are not the worse person in the world! Sure, you've made some bad judgment calls, taken some pretty foolish chances, created some awful situations, but you give yourself too much credit. Others have done far worse.
Iyanla Vansant

THERE IS NOTHING WRONG WITH YOU!

The first duty to love is to *Listen--listen to yourself, listen to all creation around you, AND listen to the person you want to love.*

To develop love in your life, you must **accept** yourself. As part of accepting yourself, you must **forgive** yourself. Of course you have screwed up. Who hasn't? It's important to realize that **we** can't forgive ourselves for existing. There is nothing to forgive. THERE IS NOTHING TO FORGIVE.

We **can** forgive ourselves for what we've done or chosen--for actions we've taken or not taken. Many years ago I had a client who struggled to do anything. She could barely get out of bed for years. She felt guilty all the time. Finally, with lots of work, she discovered the source of the guilt. Her father had sexually abused *her sister.* My client had carried the guilt of being the one he left alone; the one who survived without this horrible wound. Why didn't *she* save her sister? Why didn't *she* offer herself to her father instead? Guilt, including *Survivor* guilt can be paralyzing.

To accept and **forgive** yourself, it is necessary to practice **generosity**. If you are generous in your judgments, understanding of how someone like yourself could have screwed up, you'll more easily be able to accept and forgive your wonderfully imperfect self.

As you get better and better at doing these three skills, I guarantee you will start to notice that you are feeling the presence of love in your life. You may not know what it is at first, but you will be feeling it.

Once we are practicing acceptance, forgiveness, and generosity with ourselves, we are then able to be realistically **accountable**, first to ourselves, and then to others. Just as there are many of us who are very adept at putting ourselves down, there are many of us who have learned not to hold ourselves accountable because shame is so much a part of our judgment that we do everything we can to avoid feeling it. Challenging our shame by being accepting, forgiving, and generous allows us to hold ourselves to account for our actions, and reduces our fear of being judged by others.

It is rarely easy to be held accountable for behaviors that have somehow harmed others. Being able to do this is an important part of being able to experience love. All of us have hurt others. If we are letting go of the shame, then we can live with the consequences of our actions.

If we are able to be generous, accepting, forgiving, and accountable, then it allows us to be **vulnerable** with another person. We reduce the number of sentries standing guard at the boundaries of our heart. We allow ourselves to fully face another with our palms and arms open. We gradually become willing to share most of the deep secrets of our dreams, our fears, our possibilities.

Loving, like prayer, is a power as well as a process. It's curative. It is creative. Zona Gale

As we allow ourselves to be vulnerable, we demonstrate it through what Sternberg calls **intimate communication.** We are able to speak our secrets and generously hear another person's. Our vulnerability and open communication both imply and promote **trust** in one's self and the other. As we do this, the feeling of love becomes more and more present, more palpable in our life, increasingly, in our every moment. ***LOVE.***

If we then can have the **courage** to remain fully and *consistently* vulnerable and present for this experience, we can allow ourselves to become **humble** enough to accept this gift flowing through us as a continuing current which then increases **our commitment** to this ongoing process. ***LOVE!***

The current gets stronger and stronger as the amazing spiral of love and life moves ever and ever powerfully through every nutrino, every quark, every possibility of life. ***LOVE! LOVE! LOVE!***

Remember These Ingredients for liberating, (soulful) love:
acceptance,
forgiveness,
generosity,
accountability,
vulnerability, (intimate communication)
trust,
humility,
courage.

> *Relationship is a sacrament. Its grace is the stories it tells, the opportunities for healing it provides, and the freedom it offers.*
> K. Louise Schmidt

Remember A. J. Muste's quote at the beginning of this section--*If I can't love Hitler, I can't love at all*? Muste was a life long social justice, anti-fascist, and peace activist.

For so many of us born in the twentieth century Adolf Hitler represents the ultimate in what some would call human evil. His actions and his influence on others embody the most destructive, intense, sustained, genocidal behavior modern history has witnessed. Yet, Muste insists that the test of his own ability to love, is whether he can love this most repugnant of men--this man who caused the torture, terror, and murder of *millions* of people.

For some of us this may feel like a ridiculous test, but to Muste, who believed that we were all connected, that we were all imperfect, that we were all each more than the sum of our actions, having love for Adolf Hitler, whose actions Muste despised and actively fought against, was just what love is about. Does that seem crazy? Maybe it is. Let's carry that notion with us.

There may be simple answers to how to live a life of love, power, and happiness. However, as I hope I have conveyed, simple does not mean easy--at least at first.

There are challenges that can make the process difficult. As we continue on this journey into the heart of hurt and healing, we will explore them.

To subvert the patriarchal plot of putting boundaries on love, of calling love a scarce resource, we create instead a conspiracy to co-exist with all. Being in relation and boundless in love, without harm, requires that we all become law breakers. We need an "open eyed conspiracy," where choices in love are made with a wide awake presence of self.
K. Louise Schmidt

Medicine today focuses primarily on drugs and surgery, genes and germs, microbes and molecules. Yet love and intimacy are at the root of what makes us sick and what makes us well. If a new medication had the same impact, failure to prescribe it would be malpractice.
Dean Ornish, MD (renowned heart specialist)

Let the love that I give speak for me.

HEALING

A

SINGLE

HEART

First----Most Important:

BREATHE!!!

SLOWLY

DEEPLY

FULLY

You must remember
　　You have the right to

<u>BREATHE</u>

As we move into the heart of healing, we must allow ourselves to be alive….
Too often early trauma, early experiences of fear, teach our bodies to constrict, and then restrict our movement in so many ways.

So before we move into the **DEEP,**

Please remember to breathe

(and keep doing it)

Pay attention to YOU!

WE CANNOT HEAL WHAT WE CANNOT FEEL
John Bradshaw

You cannot fix what you will not face.
James Baldwin

Challenges

Dawn spoke to me in a monotone voice. *"I always thought he was basically a good person. He threatened me when I first left, but we'd seen each other on the street, and he was alright. I just don't know what got into him that day. It was his weekend to have Charree. So I was on the way back from the store when he come up behind me and stuck his gun in my ribs, and started rushin' me along. We walked all the way over to his place like that. I kept askin' what's goin' on. I started getting' scared for my baby. I asked him over and over again how she is, but he wouldn't answer. He wouldn't tell me about my baby. So he drags me into the house he shares with his cousin, sits me down, and makes me drink this nasty stuff. I'm sittin' there watchin' him look real funny at me, and suddenly everything is black. The next I know he's got me tied to the bed and he's doin' his nasty sh-t to me. He keeps doin' it, over and over again, the rest of the day and into the night, and I keep cryin' for my baby. He keeps punchin me and telling me to stop talkin about her.*

Finally he tells me he's going to kill me, and then he leaves, and I think I hear him go out the house. With all his shit, the ropes he tied me with were gettin loose. So after awhile I slides out of them and off the bed. I couldn't hardly stand. Blood and his sh-t all over me. I found what was left of my clothes. Somehow, I opened the bedroom door and make a run for it. And right away I trip over this rolled up rug and smash my nose, and the blood goes everywhere, but I get up and run, run so hard, I get out of that house and leap off that porch and run all the way to the 7-eleven, and they call the police for me. All the time I'm thinking 'what did that motherf--ker do to my baby!'

So here's the thing, remember that rug I tripped over? So the cops surround the house, and after awhile they go in. They don't find my ex, but in the rug they find a body. And that's how they said to me. We found a body. I freaked until they told me it was a man.

A report came over the police's radio that they found another body in a lot down the street. It was my ex. He offed himself. It was his cousin in the rug. And my baby was safe at her grandmother's. So anyway, my sister says I need someone to talk to. I don't know. I've been kind of depressed."

Remember To Breathe

Human biological systems are strong, but they are also delicately balanced. Extreme stress can throw that balance off. Our systems do whatever they can in an attempt to restore enough balance to continue functioning. Our autonomic nervous system provides us with quick methods to respond to physical or emotional stress. That includes increasing the cortisol in our body. For short periods of time this stress hormone can help. Unfortunately, when our system experiences chronic stress, excess cortisol can cause great harm. This includes impaired cognitive performance, suppressed thyroid function, blood sugar imbalances, decreased bone density, decrease in muscle tissue, higher blood pressure, lowered immunity, slowed wound healing, increased abdominal fat, heart attacks, and strokes. Fibromyalgia, an extremely painful condition that involves the contraction of the myelin sheath insulating nerve fibers, causing in some cases virtual paralysis, is often associated with the stress of chronic childhood trauma and abuse.

Our amazing systems do what they can to protect our *psyches* from harm by sometimes totally blocking the memory of events, and other times by allowing us to remember the events, but not allowing us to feel the feelings associated with the experience. While this numbing allows us to maintain a rudimentary balance, it inhibits further growth in areas of our system affected by the original event, it may make us unavailable for growth in any number of associated areas, and at times its stability may be precarious at best.

So one reader of Dawn's story might be hyper-sensitive and blend too much with her, end up highly disturbed, and perhaps not be able to continue reading this book. Another reader's systems may not allow them to feel much at all in response to the story. Often it's our own trauma history, and our level of healing that determines how much we will relate, how much we feel in response to Dawn and her story.

All of us experience traumas. Falling off the bike and breaking our arm. Being severely bullied by the kids at school. Experiencing a mom who won't talk to us when she's angry. Being physically intimidated or attacked by those who say they love us. Being mocked by peers because we appear somehow different, experiencing violence, being under attack. There are many kinds of traumatic experiences, and each person or other being will be affected in their own way by that trauma.

So many of us are wounded. So many hurting. So many of us need healing. A friend of mine, Jeffrey

Gerhardstein, wrote in a 1994 paper that all people who grow up homosexual, experience profound trauma because of the extremely hostile environment in our culture. ***Half our population***, women, grow up in an environment where as many as one in three will be sexually assaulted before the age of eighteen. According to some statistics, every twenty-one seconds another woman is battered in The United States. A third of all teen women in dating situations experience violence or intimidation. In the work place, surveys show that over forty percent of women experience sexual harassment.

No matter where I have been in the world, when walking down the street at night, hearing footsteps, never once have I turned around, fearing it might be a woman.
Attributed to Alice Walker by Evelyn White

The statistics are even worse in most of the countries around the world. Millions of women have been victim to female *genital mutilation* or *honor killings* throughout North Africa and The Middle East. The trauma is in the air these women breathe.

The FBI reports that an average of over 3,000 African-Americans are victimized by hate crimes each year. That includes murders, rapes, felonious assaults, and vandalism. Over 1,000 Jews and close to 400 Muslims are victimized by these crimes. Over 1300 Gay and trans-gendered folks are victimized. How does this victimization affect us? You? Our culture?

Home of The Brave

Jenn tells the story of being a small child observing her mother while she watched the television set as the birth dates for the draft lottery during the Vietnam War came on the screen. Jenn's oldest brother, Tim, was home from the war, and almost never left his bedroom. Her second oldest brother was eligible for the draft. Jenn watched as her mother cried, realizing that her second son's birthday had been listed early. Jenn's not sure how as a seven year old she knew to go to her mother, stroke her arm, and tell her, *"It's okay, Mom, Jimmy will be okay,"* but that's what she remembers doing.

Jimmy is evidently "okay." He joined the navy, stayed safe, and now, almost forty years later, is a grandfather, close to retirement. Jenn's oldest brother, Timmy, spent the next thirty years in and out of psych wards, treatment programs, and the veteran's hospital, being diagnosed with schizophrenia, post-traumatic stress, and alcohol and heroin addiction. He was arrested for attacking his mother and father. Arrested for beating his wife.

Finally, I guess he just gave up. My dad found him at his apartment. He had been dead for days. It was so hard. We'd all spent so long trying to help him.

My ex even got him a job at his place. And then Timmy got in an argument with the boss, and threatened him. Jenn grimaced. *My whole life, I never knew him any different. I don't remember my brother any way except messed up.*

How many people have grown up as siblings of mentally disabled or physically challenged children? While usually the person who suffers most profoundly is the one experiencing the disability, ***everyone*** in the household experiences both direct and vicarious trauma.
Jenn began to cry, *And now he's dead, and he's been dead. And I still can't help him.*

Millions of children will go to sleep tonight, one of many nights, hungry. Between 15,000 and 30,000 children will die of hunger related diseases today. How do those deaths affect their surviving siblings? How do those deaths affect their mother? Their father? You? Me?

Breathe......

Let yourself feel
       Let yourself heal
              Let yourself flow

Breathe ....

Deeply….. Slowly…. Fully…

"HEY RIVER, I thought this book was supposed to be uplifting. You are really bringing me down. This stuff is way too intense."

I'm sorry about that, ……sort of.

My mother seemed happy to me most of the time when I was a young child. As I aged, however, I recognized that there were many topics she refused to talk about. Many topics she avoided. Sometimes when she didn't want to talk about things she would just close her eyes and turn her head. I guess I instinctively knew that not facing reality, avoiding unpleasantness, not addressing problems between extended family members, or within our family, would not produce reliable happiness. I told my mother that I wanted to be happy, but I wanted to be happy *with my eyes open*. Through experience and research I now know that there is no substitute for facing the truth. I also know that we each *can* handle it.

This book is about traveling a path that will empower us, and help us experience a joyful happiness. Feeling pain, distress, and discomfort can certainly be part of that journey.

Do you remember how your family dealt with truth?

Try to remember three times when you faced unpleasant truths before you were an adult.

TRUTH TELLING

There is no healing alternative to recognizing and facing the truth. **Alice Miller**

In *Possessing The Secret of Joy,* Alice Walker has her character, Tashi, go back to the country where she was "circumcised." While there, she goes into a paper store, purchases paper, sits down on the spot, and makes a sign: "If you lie to yourself about your own pain, you will be killed by those who claim you enjoyed it."

While Rebecca's dad watched the pornographic movies with her, he would pinch his six year old daughter's nipples, complaining that she would never have large breasts like the women they were watching.

Rebecca came to me for counseling because, she says, she has a problem with anger. She reports sudden attacks on other women in the last three months. As she puts it, "Something just takes hold of me."
The first time I remember being aware of someone

in denial about their victimization came at the college where I taught and counseled, as Sam talked about his father to me. He talked about being grateful to his dad for teaching him how the "real world" worked. When I asked how his father did this, he told me that when he was eleven years old his dad started locking him out of the house if Sam came home too late.

I asked how long he would keep him locked out, figuring it was a half hour or an hour, thinking to myself that that was pretty mean. The young man without blinking, said, "Oh, usually no more than a day."

When he saw the look on my face, Sam explained, "It wasn't until I was twelve or thirteen that he did it regularly. Before that he'd usually unlock the door around midnight, before he went to bed, and if I was still awake, on the porch or in the back shed, I could come in then."

I asked him how his mother treated him. He said she was always nice in the morning when he came in to get ready for school.

SPARE THE ROD; SAVE THE CHILD

It was the early seventies. I was sitting in the living room, enjoying a good book. My belt was folded on the arm of the chair, next to me. I expected to use it again, soon. Suddenly, I heard screams from the bedroom.

When I entered the room, belt in hand, five-year-old Danny was on top of his little brother, Bob, punching him again. I immediately went into action. I let loose the belt, and it flashed out across his bottom. "I told you to leave him alone! Why don't you listen!"

"Go To hell!" Danny shouted through his tears as he threw a toy at me and retreated to his bed and backed up against the wall. Saying to myself that he had to be straightened out for this behavior, I pursued him, swinging the belt.

"Leave me alone!" You can't hit me!" He shouted as he threw a pillow, "You're not my father!" His words stopped me dead in my tracks. He was right, I thought; he wasn't my child, so I shouldn't hit him. I wondered, however, who really did have the right to hit Danny?

To put all this in perspective, I was a non-violent activist in the farmworkers union, in my early twenties, committed to peaceful change. I believed that I'd done what I could do to stop Danny's behavior non-violently. I had also been raised in a family where corporal punishment was a usual, "appropriate," though not constant part of discipline. In fact, I remember feeling fortunate that I was not a child in many of our neighbors' households.

It was not unusual to see a mother or father beat their child in front of us because he or she had not come when called, or had "sassed" someone, or for any of a number of real or imagined transgressions. I saw countless children backhanded because a parent thought them "disrespectful." Neither my mother nor father was immune from this behavior. I was not aware of one family where the threat of violence was not a fact of life. Of course, no one ever left a scar on my body, nor did I ever *notice* one on anyone else.

Millions of us, in thousands of neighborhoods, were getting spanked, smacked, or slapped throughout the 1950's and '60's while growing toward adulthood. It was normal. It was the usual. My mother and father simply did what their peers were doing. Violence or the threat of violence was a parent's tool to manage the family in my neighborhood.

So who were these parents who were doing this violence? For the most part, they were people who had been beaten themselves while vulnerable children. Many years later I found out that my grandfather had actually broken my mother's nose while "disciplining" her, and I wondered what his parents had done to him. How had their violence affected him? How had his violence affected my mother? How had hers affected me? What did I pass on to the children in my care?

The violence, of course, was not exclusive to home. By the time I had reached first grade, I'd seen teachers "paddle" children. I was attacked and beaten with a yardstick by a fourth grade teacher. I was jabbed, smacked, and had my hair pulled by a teacher in junior high. I was "swatted" with wooden or leather paddles by teachers dozens of times in junior high and high school until I finally refused to accept that punishment. Male teachers "playfully" punched me many times. One tried to punch me in the face. Because I had the audacity to defend myself, I was suspended from school. On the street police frequently attacked my teenaged friends and me, jabbing us with clubs, roughing us up with head slaps, pushes, and violent elbows while searching us.

Admittedly, many children were not physically assaulted by adults as often as I was, but there were many I knew who were victimized a lot more. More importantly, ***almost all*** children in my generation grew up victimized by the *fear* of violence from an adult.

In many ways our culture has changed since my childhood school days. Throughout the ensuing decades Dr. Spock and his successor parenting experts have discouraged, though not condemned, corporal punishment as a method of discipline. Many school systems have eliminated or severely limit corporal punishment now. There are even billboards and bus placards in at least one major city proclaiming that it is never right to hit a child.

So, what about Danny and me? For weeks I attempted to "straighten him out" as he continued to pick on Bob. I just couldn't understand what his problem was. Why did he force me to hurt him so much? What was wrong with this child that he needed to be beaten like that? I found myself more and more irritated by almost anything Danny did. Eventually, his mother stopped asking me to baby-sit. Later I found out that she had been afraid I was being too violent with the children.

> *Pain and suffering are a kind of false currency passed from hand to hand until they reach someone who receives them but does not pass them on.* Simone Weil

It's hard to describe the feeling of shame that rushed over me when I heard that. I was a trained non-violent activist who couldn't be trusted to not hurt children! Fortunately, the cognitive dissonance was too much to handle. I couldn't love myself and at the same time be someone who children would have to fear. I made a commitment to never strike another child, no matter what the circumstances.

As an alternative high school teacher, counselor, and principal I kept that commitment. I've continued to keep that commitment for over thirty years now, and I've never regretted it. I also made the commitment to help parents learn methods to minimize their violence. I found that condemning parental violence, only caused the parents to disregard my advice as unrealistic. Many of the people I've worked with have neither seen the violence as wrong, nor have they believed that there was an adequate replacement.

Let us put our minds together, and see what life we can make for our children.
Tatanka Iyotanka
(Sitting Bull)

Throughout those years as a teacher and now a therapist the question has still been with me, who had the right to hit Danny? And why did *I*?

The laws of most states gave parents, step-parents, foster parents, and school officials the legal right then, and most still have it today. We adults still have the right to commit violent acts against members of this group called children. According to researchers in the 1990s, over 80% of the American public still believed that hitting "a willful child" is an act of love. *An act of love!*

When I apologized to Danny a few years ago, he minimized the damage and told me that he probably deserved it anyway. I could have said the same thing to my mother and father. They probably would have said the same thing to theirs. You might say the same to yours.

In my over twenty years practice as a therapist and my eighteen years leading groups for batterers I've heard the following comment hundreds of times: "I got hit as a child, and I turned out okay."

Did we turn out okay? Even if we did, is "okay" good enough? All the research shows that most people are more emotionally healthy and more respectful of themselves and others if they were *not* hit as children. I am more certain than ever that we all need a basic retraining, so that as parents and grandparents we can guide, nurture, educate our children to become caring, responsible, disciplined citizens. And we can do this with confidence and success, and without the threat of violence.

After working with scores of people traumatized in childhood, I've come round and round to the same conclusion: ***No one*** should have had the

Behind all the forms of mental illness there seems to lie a generalized image of the human self as darkly unworthy and no good. It is a deep fantasy and a deep conviction that gets into everything men do. William Lynch

> *Transforming abuse embodies a strong, respectful stance that we will not allow the abuse of children, of women, or of our Earth to continue unchecked. We take this stance not out of desire for violence or revenge, but out of love.* Ellen Bass

right to hit Danny; no one should have had the right to hit my mother; no one should have had the right to hit me; and no one should have had the right to hit you.

The less violence in our lives as children, the greater our chance at reaching happiness, love, and power as adults.

Whether we talk about Sam or Tashi, or Danny and Bob, or Jenn, or the so many nameless other children I mention here, or you, or me, for us to heal we must first face and feel what, as children, would have been beyond us. Our hearts may be wounded, but our hearts are strong. We can heal. We can heal.

> *Spend five minutes in front of the mirror, repeating, I can heal. I can heal. I can heal. And I will. I can heal. I can.....*

As I have written in the earlier sections of this book, we carry our childhood baggage with us unless we become fully conscious of it, and our power to let it go. That baggage *can* harm others, and usually it does.

SHAME:
You can't tell the truth about others unless you tell the truth about yourself. Virginia Woolf

(The following is from a memoir I began writing a few years ago.)

I guess I'm writing again for this book today because I don't know what else to do. Dee attacked me last week. We were at the end of our session, and I thought she was rising to leave. Instead she reached across the table and knocked my notepad into my lap. Then she moved toward me swinging. When I slid back and jumped up, she jumped back, moved toward the windows, putting her shoulder into them. Nothing broke, but she found a stick used to prop up the window and swung around with it, looking to strike me or somehow hurt herself. I pressed the emergency buzzer as I slipped behind her and pinned her to the wall. We were like that for what seemed an eternity. The police came. It took six of them to carry her off to the hospital. It was hard explaining to the police officer that this woman is multiple, and that her alter attacked me.

This week seemed to be going a little better. Then I found out Wednesday that Jane drank a cleaning agent to get the demons out, and is now in the intensive care unit. She told them that she does not have a therapist. I've been seeing her for almost a year, but therapy has been going very slowly. She's missed about forty percent of our sessions, but is coming to group regularly. She missed her last three individual sessions and the group before last week, but showed up to last group. I called the hospital but I don't have a release to talk to anyone.

Jane's only recently been able to talk a little about family and childhood stuff. Got heavily into Christianity and beat herself up with it for years. Seems to lose time, but has not been cooperative in attempting to document her days alone at home.

Lyn is back in the hospital. It seems she went to Metro emergency room because she'd gotten something in her eye. They took one look at her arms--with all the new scars--and admitted her to the psych ward. It doesn't seem to matter to them that she wasn't suicidal. She's called me three times in the three days she's been in there. They've got her really drugged up--more wasted time. Sometimes I feel like we're in a slow motion race to build up the part of her who wants to survive before she successfully ends her life.

Lyn had only been out of Lakewood Hospital a few days. It's been just two weeks since the beginning of that last stay. I'd had her admitted because she *was* trying to off herself then. She does pills when she wants to die. The cutting's punishment and emotional relief--a coping mechanism that has become addictive. For the most part, not life threatening.

I ask myself, how I'd feel if my father had beaten and terrorized me from my earliest memories. If my father had taught me that I was always wrong. If my father had taught me that *I had* no right to an opinion, that I had no right to say no. How would I feel if my mother had stood by and done nothing to stop it, and occasionally beaten me herself? How would I feel? From the time Lyn was six years old she was sexually abused by boys in her neighborhood. She recalls having sex with a couple of the fathers of the boys as a teenager, and guess what, she blames herself. She's the slut. The whore. And getting pregnant at seventeen-- she was a horrible disgrace to her family.

It doesn't matter to her that she never once wanted the sex--*she never once enjoyed it.* I have clients who feel guilty because, in certain circumstances that they did not want, they felt physical pleasure. That can cause some misplaced guilt. But hell, Lyn never even felt any pleasure, yet she is racked with guilt. She tells me she never told anyone *No!* out loud, and, therefore, it's all her fault. All her fault.

I remember I was fifteen or sixteen, I didn't have a date on a Friday night while evidently my usual buds did. I went up to the Riverside show by myself. While there, I ran into some guys I knew from the airport projects. They were raving about this girl from their neighborhood who they said gave "great blow jobs." She was in the show that night by herself, and she'd really want to do stuff with somebody like me. They suggested I just go sit next to her, and she'd do anything I wanted her to.

It's painful when I think back to my ignorant abuse. I did not want to hurt that girl. I wanted to have a good time. I didn't want to fail in the eyes of the guys from the projects. I sat down next to her, put my arm around her. She didn't move away; she didn't protest. I kissed her. She kissed me back unenthusiastically. I put my hand on her breast. She didn't pull it away. I pushed my hand in between her legs. She opened them slightly. No protest. Not a sound. I put her hand on my lap. She didn't do anything, but she didn't move it. I didn't understand. But I knew this didn't feel right to me. I don't mean (as much as I wish it were so) it didn't feel *morally* right. It just somehow felt unnatural to me. A horrible foreboding swept over me. There was something wrong. I got up and walked away.
I never said a word to that young woman. She never even looked at me. She was known in her neighborhood as the slut who gave "great blow jobs."
So Lyn never said, "no."

As Elaine May said, telling the truth can be dangerous business. Without the truth, however, there can be no healing. I abused that young woman in the Riverside Theatre, as I abused many others in similar ways. I abused Danny, whether he thinks so or not. I wish I hadn't, but I *Did,* and like each of us who has committed transgressions against others, I must live with that knowledge. *And,* just as it is part of the healing journey to hold others accountable for their transgressions against me, it is part of the healing journey to hold myself accountable for my behaviors, and to remain available for others to hold me accountable.

> Remember: *I can heal. I can heal. I can heal.* ***And I am.*** *I can heal. I can heal. **And I am....***

It's hard to tell the truth about ourselves or others who have harmed us if we don't engage in other healing activities simultaneously. That is why I asked you to *BREATHE* when we began this walk through the territory of sometimes heart wrenching, painful healing on our journey into a life of love, happiness, and power.

So, what are the ingredients for this healing? As on any foraging journey, we need to pick up the seeds, the herbs, the legumes, the fruits, the grains to create the feast of life. These ingredients are similar to the ingredients for happiness and love.

SOME INGREDIENTS FOR HEALING:
1. Breathing.
2. Becoming Present.
3. Listening.
4. Feeling (hurt, sadness, anger, gratitude, etc.)
5. Practicing generosity, acceptance, forgiveness (mainly with ourselves)
6. Recognizing, facing, **holding on to** the truth.
7. Nurturing our body, our mind, and our spirit.
8. Believing in our rights and acting on them.

Each act of denial, conscious or unconscious, is an abdication of our power to respond.
Joanna Macy

So as we breathe, we can allow ourselves to pay attention to our feelings. What do you feel after reading these true tales of hurt, abuse, and terror?

These stories may be painful to read because you have never been through such horrible experiences. These stories may be painful because they remind you of your own. We have all been hurt. We have all been wounded. We *all* have the power to heal… if we first allow ourselves to feel.

To fully feel, we must be here in this moment. Then we must listen, listen to our breath, listen to our rhythm, and then listen to our heart.

With generosity towards ourselves, we can face and hold *whatever* the truth may be. (And perhaps make some nurturing soup out of it.)

CARING FOR OUR BODIES

When we do good things for our bodies, we are doing good things for our spirit, our mind. When we practice stress reducing, endorphin creating activities, they help our muscle, our balance, our endocrine system, reduce cortisol, and so on.

Whether that activity includes yoga, or walking, or swimming, or running, or bicycling; whether it includes learning a discipline like Tai Chi, the activity affects much beyond our immediate physical presence.

Other activities such as meditation help our total system. For some people meditation is a spiritual experience. They believe they experience guidance from a *higher power* during the activity. For others, it simply reduces stress or increases needed focus. There are basically three ingredients that must be present for successful meditation. Most meditations involve focusing on the present moment, letting the voices in your mind go quiet, and allowing, as a result of the first two, an altered state of consciousness. As meditation reduces activity in some parts of the brain, it actually *increases* activities in an area associated with positive thoughts and emotions. Some researchers argue that regular practice of meditation brings sustained positive changes in this area.

- Think about nothing now.
- Stop listening to those voices.
- Let your mind drift on.

So, how do you do this?

There are many ways to meditate. Here are some basic techniques.

Find yourself a comfortable, quiet place, get in a comfortable position. Remember to breathe slowly and deeply. Spend a moment becoming an observer of your thoughts. Don't engage in that conversation about your rising gas bill. Just observe that you're thinking about it. Now, as each thought comes up, hear it, then let it move on. Stay with the space for a few moments. Before you know it, you'll be thinking of------Nothing. Each time you do this, it will likely get easier.

Focused Meditation allows you to focus on something. It could be your own breathing. It could be a philosophical concept like universal acceptance. It can be an object in your field of view, or a repetitive or constant sound such as a running river. It still provides the opportunity for staying in the now and ignoring the buzz of conscious thought.

Activity-Oriented Meditation allows you to

focus on your actions. Yoga or Tai Chi would be considered repetitive trance producing activities, as running, swimming, and walking can be. Creative art/craft work can also produce this.

DANCE! DANCE!! DANCE!!!

Have you danced yet today? Have you moved your body to some stimulating rhythm in your heart or your gut or your head?

Among the greatest gifts my father passed on to me was the sway of his hips. While he never danced in public, my dad would regularly put a record on his hi-fi and walk through the apartment or house swaying. I was mesmerized by the way he moved. Finally, at about ten years old I realized I could move the same way, and I haven't stopped moving since.

Dance is a method to celebrate with others, and a method of worship and prayer for many. It is also a method to live in the now, to celebrate the moment within ourselves, to reduce stress, and to meditate. We can dance in the kitchen; we can dance in the car; we can dance in the hallway, the living room, the grocery store, the bank line. Moving our shoulders or moving our feet, moving our pelvis or moving our arms or our

fingers, our eyebrows--all dancing.
DANCE!!!!!!!!!

> Think of three pieces of music you like to dance to. Be sure to dance to one of them today or tomorrow.

AN APPETITE FOR HEALING

What we breathe, what we drink, what we eat matters. It matters to our physical health; it matters to our emotional health; it matters to our spiritual health; and it matters to the planet.

While we have only limited control over the quality of the air we breathe (more about this later), each of us has our own unique relationship to food, based on our access, our individual biology, our self concept, and our understanding of the universe.

In most people's lives food represents much more than sustenance. It has meaning for us on cultural, familial, and personal grounds. Food is associated with national traditions and religious rituals over the whole globe. It's also associated with family traditions, family stories. It also has different meanings to different people in the same family.

I come from a family of overeaters. The most powerful and respected man in my childhood was my mother's father: Big Grandpa. *Big* Grandpa.

He was at least two hundred pounds overweight, and wielded a lot of negative heft. All of his children were overweight, though none to the extent that he was. Most of the children of my generation ended up overweight--a handful toxically obese.

As in many households, food represented love. Almost the first comment upon entering one of the family households was, "What would you like to eat?"

In some families, people are deprived of food, and, therefore; develop a pattern of craving. In other families, like mine, food is pushed on people, and people end up craving it. In the same families other members may react by not wanting to eat. It's all about how the issues affect the *individual*, and what unique strategies each of us develops to cope.

What's your family relationship with food? What's yours? What important food rituals do you practice?

Susan, an old client of mine was bulimic. She alternated between immediate barfing after a meal, and obsessive laxative use. At the time I worked with her she had spent her whole life pre-occupied with her weight. I met her children, and her son was toxically obese, and her daughter was in treatment for anorexia. Her husband was an exercise addict. Overweight, he would binge eat, and then over exert himself attempting to burn off the calories. Susan's and her daughter's problems were not just in relation to their food. *Body dysphoria* was also present.

Growing up in a sexist society where women's value is so often determined by the shape of their bodies, most women develop some level of preoccupation with how they appear. For some, that preoccupation may lead to obsession and total dysfunction.

Much humor in our culture has come out of the heterosexual male/female contrast. *He'll wear anything. She takes forever to get ready. She's always primping,* etcetera. The unfortunate reality is that women spend tens of millions of dollars every year on cosmetic surgery. A typical woman executive spends five times as much for her clothes as a male executive. In study after study we have seen that women are judged much more on their appearance than men are. So, to some degree the body dysphoria that contributes to many women's distorted relationship with food is simply an artifact of sexist oppression.

I don't know all the back stories of the millions of folks with food problems. However, I do know this: **There's nothing Wrong with them.** They simply have some relational problems with food or their bodies that get in the way of leading a healthy life.

Unfortunately, most of us have some level of those same problems.

As I'm sure you've heard, obesity and overweight are national epidemics. Cardiovascular disease remains one of the chief causes of death for every group of adults in our society--across all ages, genders, races, and classes.

Some interesting facts about people, food, and health:

There are Carnivores, Omnivores, Herbivores.
We *humans* are omnivores. That means that our biological system allows us to digest and reap necessary nutrients from a variety of sources.*

Preconceptions limit perceptions. Seeing is believing, but we often see only what we believe.
Dean Ornish

Carnivores (lions, wolves, sharks, etc) cannot be sustained without a primarily animal based diet.

Herbivores (rabbits, chickens, horses, bovines, sheep, etc.) cannot be sustained without a virtually exclusive plant based diet.

*Our digestive systems and our cardiovascular systems work at optimal levels when our intake is a plant based diet. We can eat meat, poultry, or eggs, but they will *harm* or *kill* us even as they provide us with some of the nutrients we need.

In dozens of studies it's been found that the more a country's citizens consume meat and dairy products, the higher the incidence of breast, colon, prostate, kidney, lung, and uterus cancer, and the higher the incidence of obesity, adult onset diabetes, high blood pressure, **osteoporosis**, kidney stones, gallstones, and cardiovascular disease.

A study from the 1990s showed that the three nations with the greatest intake of dairy products also had the *greatest* incidence of osteoporosis.

The Food and Drug Administration (FDA) regulates all foods *Except* meat and poultry. Instead, The United States Department of Agriculture (USDA), the agency mandated to *promote* their sale, is also supposed to regulate them. This allows these producers to repeatedly lie to the public with no consequences other than the clogged arteries, heart attacks, colon cancers, etc. that we, the consumers will suffer.

Of eighty-four poultry inspectors interviewed by the *Atlanta Journal-Constitution* a number of years ago, *sixty* said they stopped eating chicken based on what they observed.

What we eat, and how we eat is killing us. If we are to heal, we must find a healthy relationship to food. We must face the truth about our eating patterns; we must face the truth about our food.

In recovery, we learn to feel the feelings we anesthetized with food or starved away. We become willing to experience them and take responsibility for them. Elisabeth L.

Seven Simple Steps To Improve Your Relationship With Your Food, Yourself, and Your Planet

*Listen, here's what I think. I think we can't go around measuring our goodness by what we **don't** do. By what we **deny** ourselves. What we resist, and who we exclude. I think we've got to measure goodness by what we embrace, what we create, and who we include.* From the movie *Chocolat* (Harris & Jacobs)

1. **Become** Conscious. **Stay** Conscious
   Challenge yourself to be present and available to fully taste what you eat
   Challenge yourself to be fully aware of your natural place in the cosmos *as* you eat.

2. **Embrace** challenges to your understanding of your food and yourself.

3. **Face** the truth as fully as you can. **Stay** out of ***denial.***

4. **Be** Accepting, **Be** Forgiving, and **Be** Generous with yourself (again, again, and again).

The only foods you need to release are those that are harmful to you in some way: foods you obsess over, that are nutritionally inferior, and that inhibit the clear head and clear heart you need to allow love to enter your life.
Victoria Moran

5. **Be** rigorous in doing your inventory (not punitive--remember #4).

6. **Practice** love towards your body in all its beauty and uniqueness.

7. **Work** to enjoy every bite and to become a responsible member of this eco-community we call Earth.

Let us thank the powers that be for the delicious bounty, and let us bless our joy with what Jean Watkins calls *focused awareness* as we take that next juicy bite.

HEALING ENERGY

As presented in traditional Chinese medicine, meridians are invisible channels through the body that carry energy to every organ and system. They are similar to the wiring of a house, or the veins and arteries through which our blood flows, except that they have no discrete physical structure. They run through our physical bodies but they cannot be dissected or found surgically. Meridians are part of the body's subtle energy anatomy.

They relate to each of the body's organs and system, and can be used to assess and to improve health using a variety of techniques. Acupressure and acupuncture have become accepted compliments to Western medical techniques. Reiki and the Emotional Freedom Technique (EFT) have not yet attained such full acceptance.

The word **Reiki is made** of two Japanese words - Rei which means "God's Wisdom or the Higher Power" and Ki which is "life force energy". So Reiki is actually "spiritually guided life force energy."
Reiki opens up and increases the power of healing energy flowing through the meridians. This hands of light treatment can create a sense of a deep radiance flowing through and around you. Some possible beneficial effects include relaxation, feelings of peace, and a sense of wellbeing. Some report extraordinary results. Some believe that it is effective in helping virtually every known illness and malady. It also works in conjunction with all other medical or therapeutic techniques to relieve side effects and promote recovery.

EFT teaches people to heal ourselves emotionally by using a method of tapping on meridian points as we restructure our beliefs and our narratives about ourselves.

As a scientifically oriented soul, and an experienced researcher, I look for verifiable evidence of a method's effectiveness. There is an inadequate number of replicable, controlled studies proving the efficacy of either of these methods. However, I have heard scores of testimonials from people I respect, including clients whose results I have witnessed, that confirm the apparent effectiveness of these two energy treatments.

THE HEART OF FEAR

If we are to move through our healing, we must first reach into the heart of our fear.

FEAR

Fear of the unknown, fear of pain, fear of shame, fear of being alone, fear of nothingness... .

When Tammy was growing up she was terrified of her basement. The bathroom with her bathtub was down there. It was a major act of courage for her to reach the bottom of the stairs, and then she would have to race to get to the other side of the bathroom door, so *THEY* wouldn't get her.

I remember the basement in our apartment complex when I was a child. Actually, though it was all one building, every two apartments had their own basement with an outside entrance down an unlit set of stairs. I was not supposed to go down there because the rats and other terrible things were there, *and* it was usually dark. The strings hanging from the bare light bulbs were never long enough for me to reach.

As part of the usual male rituals, older boys would grab me and throw me into one of the basements and hold the door closed until my screaming and cursing would either draw adult attention or the boys moved on to other activities of torment.

It's not difficult for me to conjure up now a distant echo of the terror I felt a half century ago. The feeling on my skin, the adrenaline spiking through my body, the dry, metallic taste in my mouth.

Fortunately, one of my older friends, whose family migrated from coal mining country, wasn't so scared of the basement. Together, we started using my basement for activities. We set up boxing matches and Halloween horror houses down there. We even put on little shows. The dark corners still gave me the *heebie jeebies,* but the basement gradually became just one more space for fun each day.

I didn't know it at the time, but I was learning something I would carry with me the rest of my life.

***It is not because things are difficult that we do not dare, it is because we do not dare that things are difficult.* Seneca**

As I grew older and witnessed violence, had guns

shot at me, knives put to my throat, faced imminent death or pain, I don't remember ever feeling any more scared than I was in the dark, unknown basement at eight years old.

In most cultures our symbolism consistently compares light with what's good, what's true, with safety, with healing. Darkness seems to represent ignorance, evil, danger. Why? There have been many theories. One common one posits that because humans are so dependent on our eyesight for functioning, and because our eyes cannot compensate for darkness very easily, it creates a sense of vulnerability and danger to our physical being. It also represents something physically/psychologically/spiritually beyond that. For some it's *the void,* the nothingness of non-existence. We don't want to be *in the dark*, about anything. Nobody wants to live in *The Dark Ages*…..

The simple fact is that most sighted people consciously depend much more on our sight for survival than we do our hearing, our taste, our touch, our smell. We are visually/spacially oriented. Our sight creates the context for our body in the world.

There are countless species of insects and animals who live quite comfortably in absolute darkness, whether at the bottom of the sea or deep within the earth.

I've worked with people blind from birth, and people either suddenly or gradually losing their sight. Those who feel most comfortable, with minimal apprehension are those who never experienced sight. From the beginning of their lives their other senses took care of them.

Still, it is difficult for us to let go of the imagery of light and dark, (*Let me shed some more light on this subject.*) In fact there was a recent novel and film in which almost everyone in the culture suddenly went blind, and it threw the culture into total disarray. Darkness does indeed SCARE us.

That doesn't mean we can't overcome or integrate that fear, and the many others we each may have, into the texture of our lives. Susan Jeffers wrote a wonderful book many years ago, Feel the Fear and Do It Anyway, which allowed readers to acknowledge that there are things we fear, but that we can also walk through that fear.

Fear is a healthy and natural feeling triggered by our nervous system, based on our brain's interpretation of our situation. For instance, I suddenly hear a number of small explosions. My system immediately reacts with a startle response. Based on what my brain tells me, that may or may not become a fear response. If this is between June 20th and July 10th, and it takes place in my current neighborhood, I will probably not experience any fear because I know that a lot of firecrackers are being set off during that time, and my brain will quickly conclude that they are the source. If, however, I am walking down an unfamiliar street in a reputed high crime area, you can bet I will feel some fear.

Fear can also come out of personal experience, trauma, and memory. For instance, when I see a police car behind me as I'm driving, I experience an overwhelming feeling of apprehension. Why? After all, the worst result is likely to be no more than a ticket for some minor infraction. However, my personal memory gives me a different message based on my experience as a teenager. This comes up before I can rationalize about the ticket.

As mentioned earlier, **like many working class teenaged city kids,** I was punched, pushed, kicked, slapped, jabbed with nightsticks, and threatened with injury and incarceration scores of times by the police on the street. Over forty years later it is those traumatic memories that flood in, before my brain has the opportunity to bring me to the present. Once I'm able to be present, I can use self-talk, based on the current reality, to reduce my apprehension.

Unfortunately, our culture can also play a part in promoting a sense of fear. For instance, according to FBI statistics, the incidence of violent crime per capita in our country peaked around the early **1970's**. With the exception of rape (which is overwhelmingly committed by someone the victim knows) and domestic violence, violent crime has been on a relatively steady **decline** for well over thirty years. In spite of that, surveys show that our citizens are far more afraid of violent crime today than they were then. Why?

Certainly, some of this fear is caused by the twenty-four hour, non-stop TV news cycle. We hear about the same cases of violent crime over and over again, packaged anew for each time slot and each network. The old newspaper adage, "If it bleeds, it leads," (meaning that gore and tragedy draw attention) has become "If it bleeds, that's all we need." TV and radio news, which used to be perceived as a public service, has become a revenue center, competing for ratings, so the marketers can raise the price for commercial time. Therefore, programmers and editors must always keep what sells in mind as they program the news departments' material.

If we examine the video game market, commercial films, or commercial television fare, the reinforcement of the world as an unsafe place is *profound.* In just a few years of watching television or films, a child or adult can see thousands of characters violently murdered. In a few years of regular video game use a player can not only witness thousands of violent character deaths, but actually be rewarded again and again for causing them; thereby being reinforced with the notion that the solution to most perceived danger in the world is to violently respond to it.

The priorities of the culture matter too. Since the development of the military-industrial complex after the Second World War, our society has become the most militarized democracy on Earth. Encouraged by amoral corporate behavior, we spend more on weapons systems, army supplies, munitions, etc. then the next twenty countries *combined*. Rather than being simply judicious, our national consciousness seems to be *preoccupied* with the notion that we have something to fear from the other nations of the world.

We now know that our leaders and our foreign policy experts, and their counterparts in The Soviet Union, regularly misinterpreted the intentions and motives of their adversaries during The Cold War. Each assuming the most vile and threatening actions from the other. Why? Because both groups were operating out of a mindset of **FEAR**.

Of course the actual issues over which there was a struggle were important ones. Political freedom, economic freedom, human rights, and the rule of law do matter. **Yet**, it was precisely because of the misperceptions, fueled by the fear, and a false *good versus evil* competition projected by both sides, that we were in such danger. All these years later, we still have enough nuclear warheads to destroy every city in the world. WHY? **FEAR**

> *When I dare to be powerful--- to use my strength in the service of my vision, then it becomes less and less important whether I am afraid.*
> Audre Lourde

It is the same mistake American leaders make when they demonize/deify a handful of people in the religious--criminal--political conspiracy that Al Qaida represents. Yes, this small group represents a threat to Americans. However, individual Americans have a greater chance of being hit by lightning *twice* than we have of being a victim of one of their terrorist acts. **FEAR**

The nineteenth century American humorist, Josh Billings said, *It's not that Americans are ignorant; it's that they know so much that just aint so.*
We have literally been manipulated into living a life of fear by our own lack of consciousness. We don't have to continue living that life.
Whatever you are afraid of, you can handle. You are strong. You are powerful. Whether it's the

Are you crazy? The fall will probably kill ya. (Butch Cassidy to Sundance after being told that the kid won't jump off a cliff into the river because he can't swim.)

darkness, or pain, or shame, or chaos, or isolation, you may be afraid, but you will move through it, and the sun will rise again.

Take a deep, deep breath--from your gut ……...Let it out slowly,   very slowly….

FEAR.
Fear grows out of the things we think; it lives in our minds. Compassion grows out of the things we are, and lives in our hearts.
Barbara Garrison

Let the fear move through you as you move through it. You can do it.
       It's
           Time
                To
      Let it   gooooooooooooooooooo

Let the waves carry you.
      The fear is just a
thought.
Find your love.
      That is where your heart belongs.

DEATH, GOD, LOSS, and FEAR:
Celebrating The Sacred Mother of The Waters

So here's a joke astronomers and physicists tell to each other:
"So a nutrino walks into a black hole...."

Geez! Talk about a void, a nothingness.

Here's another one: *Who always knows what time it is?*
A Dog, just ask him. "Now! Now! Now!" What time is it, Boy? "Now! Now!"

Just what time is it, anyway? What day? What year? Where are we, Man? We forget that these measurements are not *reality*, but rather just agreements on how to explain reality.
It's only been a century since the time zones have been accepted. Before that every town decided on it's own time. It's only been a few hundred years since the West generally accepted January as the beginning of the year. Before that each new year started in the Spring. It may be 2009 to you, but to many Muslims it's 1430, to many Chinese it's 4707, to many Iranians it's 1387, and so on.

For thousands of years, when Chinese cartographers drew maps of the world, China was always drawn at the center. When the Greeks and the Romans drew maps, guess what? The Mediterranean Sea was at the center. The word *Babylon* means *Door of the Gods*. Out of this door supposedly came all of human civilization. Why is *North* always depicted as *Up* on our maps?

Human beings operate out of what's known as the *Omphalos Syndrome*. Omphalos is the Greek word for navel. No matter who we are, no matter where we are, we tend to experience ourselves as being at the center of the universe. On the surface, this may sound like a negative thing. It may not be; it may be just the natural consequences of our biology at this time in human development. Maybe.
People talk about someone who is selfish, or not understanding, or stingy with their time as being *self-centered.* Actually, the more *naturally* self-centered we are, the more likely we will respect ourselves *and others.*

When we are *unnaturally* self-centered, we are likely to think of ourselves as better than others. We perceive others as there to serve us. We also don't experience their perspective of the world as valid. Anne Wilson Schaeff argued many years ago that there are many reality systems. problem for us is that members of the *White Male* reality system think that theirs is the only one.

While arresting non-violent activists, a southern

sheriff once said to civil rights worker, Julian Bond, "Son, it's just a case of mind over matter. I don't mind, and you don't matter."

Take the case of Mount Chomolungma--the highest land based mountain in the world. The people who live in the foothills and beyond, in Tibet, named the mountain, *Sacred Mother of The Waters* in their language a long, long time ago. The name refers to the fact that so much of the sustaining water in the life of the inhabitants flows down from this mountain. The people who live in Nepal on the other side of the mountain call it Mount Sagarmatha, *Goddess of The Sky.*

There is no way to know who first climbed this mighty edifice. The mountain was there long before the humans came. Many of the old stories have not been told in The West. A full ascent of Mount "Everest" by Western climbers was first accomplished in the early 1950's. The new name was given by European geographers as a tribute to the Englishman who measured the mountain. I'm not sure what the people who live there think about foreigners renaming their sacred mountain. The mountain already had two good names.

When the rulers of nations conquer or dominate others, it is mostly about an *unnatural*, distorted self-centeredness. When rulers and citizens of nations enslave others, when rulers and citizens of nations commit genocide, it is based on a philosophy of assumed superiority. And this is based on an unnatural self-centeredness, fueled by the same *fear* with which all humans tangle. Instead of coming to peace with the limits of ourselves, the dysfunctional cultures promote ongoing avoidance through a false mastery of the universe. As a result, both the oppressor peoples and the oppressed end up suffering, though the latter pay a much greater price.

Everyone who makes generalizations is wrong.

Hmmmmmmm

No one lives forever?

With our limited human research abilities, we have found one being that may well live forever. Earth's only immortal appears to be Turritopsis Nutricula, a jellyfish like hydrozoan, native to the Caribbean.

These interesting beings mature until they have offspring through a process called Trans-differentiation. Once they're done, they convert **back** to their juvenile selves, and start life all over again. Repeating this process over and over.

None of *my* friends or family have been able to do

this. So, I have had to conclude that immortality is also not in *my* future. However, I have heard of a kind of extended life-span belief system that exists in some cultures around the globe. The belief is that when we expire, we are not yet dead. We remain alive until everyone who knew us has also *shuffled off this mortal coil.* Because we were a part of their lives, they carry us forward with them.

Whatever our beliefs, most of us have issues surrounding death. And, we each develop methods to contend with those issues. Some of us follow religions that espouse reincarnation. Others preach the notion of a heaven and hell--with a separation of the soul from the body. Others believe that we are what we are completely now, and when we expire-cease to breath, have no brain activity, no heart beat, we are no more. Others similarly argue that though our consciousness does not go on, our energy does.

> *If we take eternity to mean not infinite temporal duration, but rather timelessness, then eternity belongs to those who live in the present.* Ludwig Von Wittgenstein

Whatever our beliefs, part of healthy healing is to come to some sort of peace with ourselves about dying and accepting loved ones' deaths. All of us will surely experience the former, and almost all of us will experience the latter.

When someone we love dies, no matter what our beliefs, unless s/he was in extreme pain, we are usually devastated by the loss.

What do you believe about an afterlife? Does it give you comfort?

God grant me the serenity to accept the things I cannot change; courage to change the things I can; and the wisdom to know the difference.

Living one day at a time; Enjoying one moment at a time; Accepting hardships as the pathway to peace.

Most of this prayer is famous the world over, any place where recovering addicts gather. The Christian philosopher Reinhold Niebuhr wrote those words early in the twentieth century, and early AA adherents made them a base of their philosophy of recovery.

For those who believe in "God," this prayer seeks his/her support for acting out of a healthy reality base which helps in leading an effective life. It encourages courage, thoughtful judgment, and, so importantly, *acceptance.* It reminds us of the limitations of our power.

We are, each one of us, at every moment, a heartbeat away from death. Seen against this backdrop of our certain mortality, our differences are dwarfed by our commonality--and the importance we hold for one another. Ira Byock

Dr. Ira Byock, a long time advocate for improving care through the end of life, tells us about what he thinks are the four things that matter most, in his book by the same name. In his decades of working with people at the end of life and their families, he has concluded that the four simple phrases, *Please forgive me, I forgive you, Thank you,* and *I love you* are necessary to complete any significant relationship, and are extremely important to our journeys on the path to emotional healing.

Please forgive me.
I forgive you.
Thank you.
I Love You.
                ***I Love you.**ns*
                            I LOVE YOU!

Making peace with ourselves, with our loved ones, with those we have harmed, with those who have harmed us, can be a daunting proposition at times. **Letting go** of the resentments and buried guilt frees us for love, frees us to move on, even if that moving on is into death or living with the loss of another. As a rule, those who had unhappy, painful relationships with parents or partners, have a much harder recovery from their grief if they don't make an effort to let go of the resentments and guilt.

I forgive you	*Please forgive me*	Look at the person in the mirror, and repeat these at least five times.
Thank you	*I love you.*	

Mortal Mystery

I searched for God and found only myself. I searched for myself and found only God. **Sufi proverb**

We do not see things as they are. We see them as we are.
The Talmud

I've seen too much magic in my life to not believe in it, but where does it come from? Philosopher Josiah Royce wrote early last century about a "larger self." Essentially, he was arguing that we are all connected through a kind of mental energy of which most of us simply aren't aware. This connection forms the larger self, a beloved community, and a kind of *higher power* that we can access as we move on our individual journeys. Or maybe the magic comes from Krishna, or Kali, or Jehovah, or Shiva, or Hathor, or Mari. Maybe. What do you believe?

> *It all comes down to this.*
> *We've got to walk through our fear,*
> *Step into the abyss./Take hold of the love,*
> *Let go of the rest,/Cuz it all comes down to this.*

In the end, Joan Borysenko sums up the issue:

The question is not whether we will die, but how we will live.

That's the story. Live each moment as though it's our first. Live each moment as though it's our last, because each of these moments is sacred.

*Now I understand that "sacred" is just another way of describing what is **most** special and therefore, the **most** fun, the **most** meaningful, the **most** intimate, the **most** erotic, the **most** exciting, the **most** powerful, the **most** joyful, the **most** playful, the **most** friendly.* Dean Ornish

Making Choices

It is difficult to lead a full, healing, happy life without creating **GUIDING PRINCIPLES** for ourselves. This code of ethics is sometimes supplied to us by our religion. Most major faiths have at least some edicts that are meant to help their adherents live an honorable life. If we learn to reflect on these principles and actually take conscious ownership of them rather than simply follow them, these edicts can be very useful. However, a thoughtful code of ethics, a set of guiding principles, must live within one's own heart if they are to be of value to growth, healing, and happiness.

These guiding principles give us a compass as we move along on our journey. What are we committed to? What will we sacrifice for? What are we willing to die for? What kind of values do we want in our friends, our family? What will we teach our children?

> *May your strength give us strength may your faith give us faith, may your hope give us hope, may your love bring us love.*
> Bruce Springsteen

Thou shall not steal.
Thou shall not kill.
Thou shall not lie.
Thou shall treat others as you wish to be treated yourself.
Judge not, lest ye be judged.

This is just a sampling of some common principles to which many of us aspire.

Now, even if we have firm values, clear principles, it's important to recognize that life is not always simple enough to fully act on them.

> *I felt like the weight of the universe had been lifted off my heart.* Capt. Sullenberger, after he found out, following many hours, *that the count was 155.* (Every person in the plane he landed in the Hudson River had survived.)

Thou shall not kill is an edict promoted in almost every culture, but what about war? What if your group is oppressed by another? Would you kill to free your people? Many who believe killing is wrong, support capital punishment. How? One should not steal, but what about when your children are starving and you have no way to get work? People should tell the truth, but what if you know telling the truth will hurt the person you tell? People should not cheat on their partners. If they're unhappy and have no hope for the relationship, they should get a divorce or leave, but what if they're victims of domestic violence and believe they will be killed or their children will be taken by the abuser if they get a divorce? Should they not allow themselves to experience emotional support and intimacy which might actually empower them to challenge their oppression?

You got to stand for something' or you'll fall for anything at all.
John Mellencamp

One should not steal, but what about driving the company car to the corner for a quick run to the store, or using the company cell phone for a few calls? You're not really stealing, right?

What's important to you? What behaviors or values do you hold most dear?

One of the beauties of life is that there are rarely any absolutes. Our commitment must be to making conscious, thoughtful decisions, using our principles to guide us; knowing we are, indeed, imperfect, but delightful, unique creations--with each moment a chance to learn, grow, and decide who we will be.

What values are unacceptable in a friend?

THE HEART OF KINDNESS

If I can stop one heart from breaking, I shall not live in vain. **Emily Dickinson**

A pessimist, they say sees a glass of water as half empty; an optimist sees the same glass as half full. But a giving

person sees a glass of water and starts looking for someone who might be thirsty. If you don't, who will?
G. Donald Gale

Around 1983, peace activist Anne Herbert coined the directive, *Practice Random Acts of Kindness and Senseless Acts of Beauty.* In 1993 Conari Press published *Random Acts of Kindness*, a book of stories demonstrating kindness. Soon after, the Random Acts of Kindness Foundation was established. It's purpose is to be a resource for people committed to spreading kindness. They provide a wide variety of materials on their website, including activity ideas, lesson plans, project plans, a teacher's guide, project planning guide, publicity guide, and workplace resources to promote kindness–all free of charge.

I am still learning --how to take joy in all the people I am, how to use all my selves in the service of what I believe, how to accept when I fail and rejoice when I succeed.
Audre Lourde

Perhaps the greatest story ever told is the one about the last act of kindness in which you were involved.

The local daily newspaper in Cleveland, *The Plain Dealer*, has developed a feature called *Thankful Thursday*. Once a week on the inside of it's front page the paper prints letters from readers who want to give thanks to someone. They read like this:
I'd like to thank the young lady who stopped to see if I needed help on I-90 after I hit a deer. Rocky River

I'd like to thank the young woman who drove me home from the Giant Eagle in a pouring rain, and refused to take any money.
Brunswick

The beginning and end of Torah is performing loving acts of kindness.
The Talmud

Thank you to the older gentleman who helped me fix my son's car seat in the parking lot of Panera's on Saturday morning.
Cleveland Heights

We would like to thank Melanie, who overheard that we were celebrating our fortieth anniversary at the Brick Chimney, and paid for our dinner without us knowing it. *Garfield Heights*

A big thank you to the man who walks every morning on Lake Avenue. Each morning he greets me with a big smile and a great hello. He just makes my day. *Lakewood*

Let the beauty we love be what we do. Rumi

This, of course, is a community gratitude list. The paper gives people the opportunity to express gratitude. It is also a small, healthy sample of random acts of kindness performed by members of the Greater Cleveland area. *The Plain Dealer* provides a very valuable service to Cleveland community members by reminding us of the many kinds of kindness being performed every day, every hour, every moment of our lives.

I see life as both a gift and a responsibility. My responsibility is to use what God has given me to help his people in need. **Milliard Fuller (Habitat for Humanity)**

The foreclosure Angel, Marilyn Mock, who bought a house and gave it back to the owner to live in, and then later established a foundation to help forclosed families, says simply, ***"Because it needs to be done."***

Catherine Ryan Hyde's novel, <u>Pay It Forward</u>, and the film based on the book, have been inspirations for millions of people around the world. The central theme in the book is what starts as a student's class project. His project is to go around doing kind deeds and requesting the recipients of his action do a kind deed for three other people: To pay it forward.
There is now a foundation by that name, dedicated to helping students and others learn to develop projects that show this generosity.

As a historian, I can't help mentioning that Ben Franklin proposed a similar idea in a letter he wrote well over two hundred years ago. Someone asked for a loan, and he asked the man to pass the money on, with the same instruction to the next recipient, rather than pay him back. That way, Franklin contended, the man would be helping him help a lot of people with a very little investment on Franklin's part.

Some Health Benefits of Kindness

Allen Luks, in his book, *The Healing Power of Doing Good: The Health and Spiritual Benefits of Helping Others,* lists a number of health benefits for us as we initiate kind acts towards others. Here are a few of those, based on a compilation by the Niagara Wellness Council.

Practicing an act of kindness

• Helps contribute to the maintenance of good health, and it can diminish the effect of psychological and physical diseases and disorders.

• May create a helper's high. Our endorphins are released after performing a kind act. We get a charge-a rush of euphoria, followed by a longer period of calm and emotional wellbeing.

• Reverses feelings of depression, supplies social contact, and decreases feelings of hostility and isolation that can cause stress, overeating, ulcers, etc. A drop in stress may decrease the constriction within the lungs that leads to asthma attacks.

• Can enhance our feelings of joyfulness, emotional resilience, and vigor.

• Decreases the intensity and awareness of physical pain.

• Reduces attitudes that negatively arouse and damage the body.

• Promotes the return of health benefits and sense of well-being for hours or even days whenever the helping act is recalled.

• Creates an increased sense of self-worth, greater happiness, and optimism, as well as a decrease in feelings of helplessness and depression.

So kindness is a profound ingredient for individual and group healing. No matter how deep our wounds, we heal a little more with each act of kindness we perform.

In the midst of winter, I found within me an invincible summer. **Albert Camus**

So often thinkers write or talk about doing for others instead of ourselves. Being selfless is a goal we should strive for. I take the position that our focus has to start with ourselves, not with an artificial selflessness. It must be an honest reality based belief that I cannot fully serve *myself* without serving *the whole of creation*.

Enlightened self interest depends on how we experience the self. If I believe I am part of our earth, that we are all part of this moving mother, then my self interest may be what I understand the best interest to be for Earth, for all the beings upon and within her, for the atmosphere that sustains them. That's my self interest. Unfortunately, when we are brought up in an atmosphere of fear, apprehension, and scarcity, it is easy to comprehend ourselves as separate; to comprehend others as strangers, rather than extended family members. As we heal ourselves, we each open our life to the possibility of a life of love and power.

Remember:
Our own pulse beats in every stranger's throat.
Barbara Deming

Healing a single heart will always be an incomplete task because our own individual hearts are never totally separate from our community of hearts, from the heart of our community, and can never be fully healed if others are suffering.

With all things and all beings let us be as family.
                                            Medewakanton saying

We are the flow, we are the ebb
We are the weavers, we are the web.... *
From an equinox ritual used by imprisoned women committing civil disobedience, Diablo Nuclear Power Plant, 1981.

A conspiracy of love that cannot be bought, controlled or regulated is growing. It calls for a boundless open heart. This involves the willingness to move from the centre to unsettled and improvised positions, and learn by heart what a non-enemy ethic means in our lives.
K. Louise Schmidt

More gratitude: I'm grateful to Little Richard and Jerry Lee Lewis for making me shake. I'm grateful for Joan Baez, Pete Seeger, Bob Dylan, Holly Near, Ani Defranco, and The Black Eyed Peas for helping me sing while I do the work I believe in. I'm grateful for The Fellowship of Reconciliation and The War Resisters League for helping me grow into the man I wanted to be. I'm grateful to Larry Bruner and his bosses for helping me stay out of prison. I'm grateful for Mary Daly, Andrea Dworkin, Caesar Chavez, Wil Nichols, and James Baldwin for helping me grow into the man I have become. I'm grateful to all the union organizers who have fought the corporations (amoral by design), and who have brought you the time to read this, and me the time to write it. I'm grateful to the guy who just told me I left my keys on the counter, and to Harry Belafonte, who helped me connect my rhythm to my brain.

HEALING THE HEART OF OUR COMMUNITY

now I swear your salvation isn't too hard too find,
None of us can find it on our own.
We've got to join ... in spirit, heart and mind.
So that every soul who's suffering will know they're not alone.
It's a simple truth we all need, just to hear and to see.
None of us are free, one of us is chained.
None of us are free. Solomon Burke

There is a story I have heard as a Buddhist tale and a Jewish one. I prefer the following version. Junie was seeking the answer to the world's troubles. He had journeyed to many lands, seeking answers from all those he encountered. Finally, he met Wise Womon, and asked what the secret to human happiness was.

Wise Womon beckoned him, "Walk with me, and we shall see."

And together they walked until they came to a small building with two rooms. In the center of the first room, upon a low fire, sat a huge pot of savory simmering stew. Junie's mouth watered as he smelled this delicious food. A group of emaciated people sat around the pot, in a circle, each of them holding a spoon with an extremely long handle. Each person could reach the pot with their spoon, but the handles were so long that every time someone dipped their spoon into the pot and tried to get it to their mouth, the stew would spill. These people were clearly hungry and miserable.

Wise Womon invited Junie to the other room, almost identical to the first. A second pot of stew simmered there, in the center of the room, and another group of people sat in a circle around it; each person with one of those long spoons. But in this room the people seemed content. They smiled and talked cheerfully with one another. They seemed well-fed, and happy, and they invited Junie and Wise Womon to share their feast.

"I don't understand," Junie was confused as they sat without spoons, "What is the secret to human happiness?"

Just then a spoon was brought to his mouth. One of the people on the other side of the circle had used her long spoon to offer Junie some food.

Wise Womon smiled, "It's simple," she said. "You see, they have learned to feed each other. Now let's go back to the other room, and see what *we* can do."

In this story Wise Womon emphasizes two issues. First, Cooperation. If we allow ourselves to experience our personal challenges as challenges that others certainly face, that we are all sisters all brothers in need, then we can open ourselves to another's desire to help us, and our desire to help them. We will *cooperate*.

Researchers at Emory University have found that while engaged in cooperation, the same part of the human brain lights up that lights up when eating chocolate or experiencing other delights. It would appear that we are hardwired, genetically predisposed, to cooperate with our brothers and sisters. It is also possible that, except when distracted by fear, we are predisposed to cooperate with all the things and beings of Mother Earth.

Wise Womon was also teaching Junie an incredibly important lesson with her final statement. "...see what *we* can do." Learning the lesson of happiness is not just for Junie's edification; it is so Junie can become part of the solution--so Junie can help his brothers and sisters in the other room change their way of experiencing the universe, too.

GENEROSITY (without consciousness)

I watched my mother a lot when I was a child. I watched her frequently welcome battered and bruised women into our home, always keeping a few dollars aside in emergency money for the local "girls" in need. She also lent out the money when neighbors were just "a little short" that week because the men had piddled it away on booze. In spite of the fact that my dad made less money than most of our neighbors, and lost a chunk of that each week gambling, my mom still kept that five or ten dollars to help those who needed it.

Unfortunately, my mother also supported the system that oppressed her and her sisters. In part, because of her own violent childhood experiences, she *always* encouraged the women who came to her to return to their drunken, abusive husbands. "Oh, he didn't really mean to hurt you, Honey. I'm sure he's sorry. The kids need him. Maybe Chucky (my dad) could go talk to him."

I don't remember my dad ever talking to any adult about anything except baseball, football, card games, or the weather. As far as I know, the women always went home to their abusers, with my mother's blessings. And my mother kept the money and the comfort ready for the next time.

Just because we can't make the world perfect, doesn't mean we can't do something to make it a little better.
John Robbins

Consciousness and Conscience

So *the secret* to happiness is not really much of a secret. Leo Busgaglia's comment about us all having the capacity to love, but not the ability, holds true with most of our life challenges. In the previous section, I wrote about the reaching out to our neighbor and our neighbor's neighbor, being kind, being generous. If we're going to remain conscious, learn to be happy *with our eyes open,* we must also look beyond the beautiful and essential act of simple kindness, and plum deep into our fundamental understanding of how our world works, how we each experience it, and how each of us can affect that process. No matter what we do, we must remember to listen. Listen to the rhythm of our own heart. Listen for the rhythm of that friend's or stranger's heart. If we're willing, we will find a way for them to beat in healthy complementary rhythms that contribute to a composition that supports the life of our planet.

RETHINKING REALITY

If we truly listen, that may mean shifting our paradigm, restructuring the way we see the world. You're probably familiar with the print that seems to be a white vase with a black background, but if you look at it long enough, it becomes two profiles, facing each other. What do you think has happened for you?

Death to Traffic! Travel guru Rick Steves heard those words from a cab driver while stuck in

Tehran traffic. Like most Americans, Steves has been hearing *Death To America,* from Iranians for the last thirty years, assuming Iranians wanted our country to die, to be destroyed. The helpful driver explained that it actually was a common phrase used in Iran toward anything that causes frustration, that seems beyond control. It doesn't literally mean that the speaker wants something dead. Death to traffic, death to the electric company, death to the heat! Steves explained, on Bob Edwards public radio show, that it made him think of a phrase he uses. *Damn those teenagers for making noise so late!* Steves knows he doesn't literally mean that those kids should rot in Hell, but a person from another culture who doesn't know how we use the language might mistakenly think otherwise. Damn those Perceptions!

It all works out in the end. In the summertime the rich get the ice; in the wintertime the poor get it. Bat Masterson, 1921

There are many things we think we know, we think we see clearly, but really don't. For instance, picture the wagon trains heading west. You've seen them in the Hollywood films. Many people died on those journeys. What was the chief cause of their deaths? Wild Indian attacks, right? We've all seen the movies. Guess what. That's not even close. Indian attacks come in a distant

Rather than seeing is believing, believing is seeing. We must believe another way of living is possible in order to see it actually taking shape around us. Frances Moore Lappé

third. The second greatest cause of death for western pioneers en-route was diseases, many of which would have befallen them even if the travelers weren't on the trail. So what in the world was the main cause of death? Water. *Water? Thirst?* No.
Since most travelers were either poor swimmers or could not swim at all, according to the travelers' diaries, hundreds died simply trying to get across rivers. Far more than from any other cause. Perceptions.

What group used scalping as a systemized method of wiping out their perceived enemies? Given the last answer, you may have surmised that this answer *is not* Indians. It *is* Euro-Americans. In most colonies, and later, states, bounties were paid for Native American scalps. Never underestimate the profit motive. In spite of what you've seen in films, Euro-Americans scalped *far* more Indians than visa versa. Perceptions.

Did you hear the one about American foreign aid? Our generous government gives more foreign aid than any other nation in the world--sort of. While we lead in actual dollars (because we have the largest economy in the world), we actually give a smaller percent of our budget to foreign aid, and a smaller amount per capita than almost any other industrialized democracy. On top of that,

historically, most of that aid has served as a welfare system for *American* defense contractors. Our tax money is given in credits to foreign governments that can only use these credits to buy weapons from *our* defense corporations. So our foreign aid tax dollars are going to expand the profits of giant American corporations, not to citizens of foreign countries.
Perceptions.

When we study the vast array of species of animals and insects living on and in the earth we find that among the overwhelming majority of these groups, the female is the dominant sex. Why then do we call it the Animal *King*dom? Perhaps you have heard of Hunter--Gatherer societies. These groups that do not settle into agricultural lifestyles, but rather travel from place to place living off the land, were classified by the same eighteenth and nineteenth century European male researchers who declared the existence of the animal *king*dom. The strange thing about the hunter-gatherer title is that ***two-thirds to three quarters*** of the food consumed by most of these groups is *gathered* plant food. The **majority** of gatherers were/are women. The **majority** of the hunters are men. Why are they called *Hunter*--Gatherers?   *hmmmmm.*
Perceptions.

> When was the last time you had an experience that dramatically shifted your ground or your perspective? Can you remember more than once?

Surely, you have heard, *They've been fighting over there (Middle East) for a thousand years,* or *The world has always been a dangerous place. There's always been war.* Any detailed reading of history and archeology shows these statements to be **nonsense**. Since the Roman empire destroyed Israel around nineteen hundred years ago, until the twentieth century, Jews lived in relative peace throughout the Arab world. While there was some serious discrimination at times, overall, Jewish life in the Muslim-Arab world was not burdened with the systemic scapegoating, discrimination, and eventual genocide perpetrated in the European world against the Jewish people. It was only after the First World War, when a dramatic increase in Jewish migration began, that conflict between Arabs and Jews slowly developed into the enmity that exists between the two groups today. This is not some ancient conflict that will never be resolved. It is a twentieth century problem that may well be solved early in the twenty-first century.

So what about this misrepresentation regarding human history and war? Without a doubt, most humans who have walked the planet have *never* experienced war or attack. Most humans in history have not had to fear violence from another human (other than family members in some cultures) against them. Because of our predisposition to measure everything through wars, and the unusual amount of violence over the last two hundred years, we have a distorted perception of history, *not* supported by research.   Perceptions.

How about this one? *You can't fight city hall!* This statement is a truism that is heard within and across groups all over the culture. The obvious meaning is that you can't fight those with government power. In reality, not only *can* you fight city hall, *you can beat it*--and citizens have, time and time again. Almost every right we have came as a result of citizens standing up against government and big corporations. Speaking truth to power. From freedom of speech to freedom against invasion of privacy, from the eight hour day, minimum wage, food and work safety, to civil rights, renters' rights, property rights, women's rights, gay rights and religious rights, it took citizens committed to action against the powers that be, to make them a reality. It isn't usually easy--look at recent events in Iran--but that doesn't mean it can't be done.

Perceptions matter. They can prevent us from actually looking at *reality*, or they can enlarge our understanding of ourselves, allow us to fully live in the real world, and encourage us to become the reflective, humble person and the active, compassionate community member we can be.

CULTURAL DENIAL

There are many forms of cultural denial. What they all have in common is *The Emperor's New Clothes* Syndrome. It's an overtly and/or tacitly agreed to acceptance of a fiction. A good example is the acceptance in industrial societies of the poison that has been spewed into our air for the last 150 years. For most of that time, even as people periodically died in London or Los Angeles smog, we ignored the problem. The fiction was that we can put all these horrible chemicals into the air, and not pay a price. For the past four decades the fiction has been that there is a problem, but we can make some small adjustments, and utilize technology to take care of the poison. Because we accept the fiction, we don't acknowledge the meaning of hundred fold increase in reports of asthma and other breathing illnesses; we don't notice the insanity that our society issues daily *air quality* reports, letting us know when it will be bad for our health if we step outside our doors. **Denial.**

Why are the missiles called peacekeepers when they're meant to kill?
Tracy Chapman

International goodwill ambassador and world championship boxer, Mohammed Ali, represents another example of denial. I was a young teenager when Ali gained fame as this beautiful, brave man who floated like a butterfly, stung like a bee, and challenged the American war machine by refusing to accept the draft. As we watched him pummel and eventually be pummeled in the ring year after year, his aura of invulnerability was heroic.

He's not so classically beautiful anymore. He's now our *feel good* athlete. As we watch him shake, hardly able to hold the Olympic torch, his speech barely audible, most of us join in the denial of what caused his Parkinson's symptoms. He is not someone who has naturally aged, not someone afflicted with an illness that could not have been avoided, but someone who entertained us with deliberate, intentional, systematic, violent bodily harm to others and himself. Ali, the other boxers, the trainers, the investors, the arena owners, the TV networks, the commercial sponsors, and the viewers all entered into our own levels of cultural denial as we made money or reveled in the pain and harm inflicted on the participants As is often the case, the culture either denies the harm, minimizes it, or declares there is nothing that can be done about it. It's not an accident that Extreme Fighting/Mixed Martial Arts presently have some of the highest ratings on cable TV. These horribly harmful behaviors are regarded as entertainment in our culture because they are artifacts of a mindset of a world that is all about scarcity and danger. A world that only exists because we choose to make it exist. A world that can't be maintained without **denial**.

TWELVE MILLION REASONS UP IN SMOKE

Convinced that this period in history would be judged one day, I knew that I must bear witness. I also knew that, while I had many things to say, I did not have the words to say them. Painfully aware of my limitations, I watched helplessly as language became an obstacle. It became clear that it would be necessary to invent a new language. But how was one to rehabilitate and transform words betrayed and perverted by the enemy? Hunger--thirst--fear--transport--selection--fire--chimney: these words all have intrinsic meaning, but in those times, they meant something else. Simon Wiesenthal

GENOCIDE   GENOCIDE   GENOCIDE

Look again at the passage by Simon Wiesenthal. Think of the atrocities committed by Nazis. Think of the despicable behavior perpetrated against Jews, Roma, other Eastern European peoples, homosexual, transgendered, and disabled people. How could they do that to other human beings? How could they be so *evil*? And what about the rest of the German population--how could they go along with it? There's no way to rationalize or justify this behavior, is there? I expect and hope, as the passage reminds you of The Holocaust, it generates a lot of outrage in you. Though it's been a struggle to stay out of denial, the German people have spent the last fifty years becoming accountable for what people did in their name.

Most of the current population was not yet born at the time of the holocaust, yet their nation is committed to *Never Again*. Successive German governments have designed permanent memorials, reminding their own people and the world not to forget. They've also become a prominent voice for human rights around the world. Some would say that's the least they could do. What do you think?

Now, read over the next three passages. How do you feel when you read them?

When we entered the cell not a sound broke the stillness. "Benjamin, Benjamin!" whispered my grandmother. No answer. "Benjamin!" she again faltered. There was a jingle of chains. The moon had just risen, and cast an uncertain light through the bars of the window. We knelt down and took Benjamin's cold hands in ours. We did not speak. Sobs were heard, and Benjamin's lips were unsealed.... He asked her pardon for the suffering he had caused her. She said she had nothing to forgive; she could not blame his desire for freedom. He told her that when he was captured, he broke away, and was about casting himself into the river, when thoughts of her came over him, and he desisted. She asked if he did not also think of God.... "No, I did not think of him. When a man is hunted like a wild beast he forgets there is a God, a heaven. He forgets every thing in his struggle to get beyond the reach of the bloodhounds. "
"Put your trust in God. ... and your master will forgive you."
"Forgive me for what, mother? For not letting him treat me like a dog? No! I will never humble myself to him. I have worked for him for nothing all my life, and I am repaid with

stripes and imprisonment.
Benjamin had been imprisoned three weeks, when my grandmother went to… his master. He was immovable. He said Benjamin should serve as an example to the rest of his slaves; he should be kept in jail till he was subdued, ….
Three months elapsed,….One day he was heard to sing and laugh…. He worked at his chains till he succeeded in getting out of them. He passed them through the bars …, with a request that they should be taken to his master, and he should be informed that he was covered with vermin. This audacity was punished with heavier chains. Those chains were mournful to hear.
Another three months passed, and Benjamin left his prison walls…. A slave trader had bought him….
Could you have seen that mother clinging to her child, when they fastened the irons upon his wrists; could you have heard her heart-rending groans, and seen her bloodshot eyes wander wildly from face to face, vainly pleading for mercy; could you have witnessed that scene as I saw it, you would exclaim, Slavery is damnable!
<u>Incidents in the life of a Slave Girl,</u> Harriet Jacobs

Breathe   deeply   fully

There were some thirty or forty squaws collected in a hole for protection; they sent out a little girl about six years old with a white flag on a stick; she had not proceeded but a few steps when she was shot and killed. All the squaws in the hole were afterward killed…. The squaws offered no resistance. Everyone I saw dead was scalped. I saw one squaw cut open with an unborn child, as I thought, lying by her side…. I saw quite a number of infants in arms killed with their mothers. Robert Bent (a mixed blood guide)

...I did not see a body of man, woman, or child but was scalped, and in many instances their bodies were mutilated in a most horrible manner--men, women, and children's privates cut out...; I heard one say he had cut out a woman's private parts and put them on a stick.... Men had cut out the private parts of females and stretched them over the saddle bows and wore them over hats while riding in the ranks. A lieutenant in The New Mexico Volunteers

BREATHE...Remember to...BREATHE

Our Euro-American biological or *cultural* ancestors were the perpetrators of those atrocities. None of us were yet alive when the most horrendous acts of these ongoing atrocities were taking place, but they were done in our name. However, The wealth of our nation, the relative availability of cheap land, and the reduced competition for jobs and credit, have all benefited Euro-Americans of the past *and* right up to the moment I am writing this. Objective sources have proven that job, credit, and housing discrimination are still widespread problems across our country. Of course, everyone of us who is not Native American has gained because of the genocide against *them*.

Incidentally, I feel absolutely no guilt, not a molecule of shame about any of this history.

While I am not responsible for the extermination policies perpetrated by The United States government against the First Peoples, or the slavery built into this nation's constitution and world view, or the systematic discrimination against African Americans by local governments all over this country in the past, I do need to ask myself, for what *am I* responsible?

While I am not responsible for the laws that kept women from owning property or voting through most of United States history, and I am not responsible for the laws in my state, Ohio, that until about two decades ago allowed a man to rape his wife, and not be charged, I do need to ask myself, what will I stand for, what will I live for, what will I fight for, what will I work for today?

> *We can start where we are. We are enough. There are no "others" to blame--each of us is the other.*
> Leo Busgaglia

Will I work to become aware of my own privilege? Will I seek to enlarge my perspective? Challenge myself to listen to my heartbeat *and* the heartbeat of all other travelers along this path? Act to support the rights and liberation of all? What am I willing to do today to reduce the suffering or add to the joy of our planet?

We who lived in concentration camps remember the men who walked through the huts comforting others, giving away their last piece of bread. They have been few in number, but they offer sufficient proof that everything can be taken away from a man but one thing: the last of human freedoms--to choose one's attitude in any given set of circumstances, to choose one's own way. Viktor Frankl

Everyday, the man responsible for the "solidarity" saved the small pieces of bread, even the really tiny ones that we took from our scanty rations, and then he distributed them among the weakest of us. I myself benefited from it and it was maybe thanks to these few crumbs of bread that I survived, and that many of us had the courage to "hold on" until the end. François Faure

I find each of the last two passages moving and inspirational. Tears come to my eyes when I think of the profound message of individual power and generosity Viktor Frankl describes.

Critically to our future and the future of the planet, the second passage illustrates that *in community* we can make a difference. How many people like François Faure survived because of that effort?

For each act of thoughtlessness, each act of deceit or greed; for each physical or sexual assault, each senseless killing that takes place, there are *tens of thousands* of acts of thoughtfulness, of kindness taking place in every moment on our beautiful planet. There are thousands and thousands of people reaching out to each other to challenge injustice, to pressure their culture and their government to move towards a healthy, functional life of consciousness, conscience, justice, and peace.

I swore never to be silent whenever and wherever human beings endure suffering and humiliation. We must always

take sides. Neutrality helps the oppressor, never the victim. Silence encourages the tormentor, never the tormented.
Elie Wiesel

"NO MORE GENOCIDE IN MY NAME!"
                                       Holly Near

Context and Conscience

Solidarity means changing the us and them to the us IN them. It is all about us. We are in this together.

Riane Eisler, in two brilliant books, <u>The Chalice and The Blade</u> and <u>Sacred Pleasure</u>, has laid out both an explanation for how our cultures have become so dysfunctional, and a cultural transformation theory that can help us come back to the path that will lead our species towards the balance the world needs.

Each act makes us manifest. It is what we do, rather than what we feel, or say we do, that reflects who and what we truly are.
Leo Busgaglia

Eisler argues, utilizing archeological, climate, general scientific, and historical research, that two general kinds of cultures existed through most of human history. **Partnership** cultures, in which there was little violence, relative equality between individuals, earth based spirituality--honoring both feminine and masculine qualities, usually no walls around the towns, and only small differences in wealth among members of the group. Some of the most respected ancient cultures, such as the Minoan on Crete, appear to have operated along these lines.

Dominator cultures are far more familiar to us today. The cultures we honor have traditionally fallen into this group. Indo-European, later Greek, Roman, later Egyptian, Babylonian, and Jewish cultures all followed a pattern that included the development of strict ruling hierarchies, rigid gender roles, wide differences in wealth, spirituality that celebrated domination and the demeaning of the feminine divine. These cultures tended toward violence, authoritarianism, with all freedom subject to those with the power to physically coerce or harm others and the Earth.

Frances Moore Lappé asks, in her book, Hope's Edge, with Anna Lappé, *Why have we, as societies, created that which as individuals we abhor?* She goes on to state:

No one would intentionally destroy so many species in just this century that it could take the planet 10 million years to recover.
No one would seek to poke a hole the size of a continent in the ozone layer, causing cancer deaths to soar.
No one would decide to create a green house effect

> *For what we are beginning to wake up to today, as if from a long drugged sleep, is that we have for millennia structured our social institutions and our systems of values precisely in ways that serve to block, distort, and pervert our enormous human yearning for loving connections.*
> Riane Eisler

disrupting life in ways we are only barely beginning to understand, or make our food production--our fossil fuel driven industrial world--into one of the biggest culprits, responsible for one fifth of human caused greenhouse gas emissions.

No one would consciously design a world community in which a few hundred individuals control as much wealth as half the world's population, and where--as it is here at home--one percent end up with more than do the bottom 95 percent combined.

This *is* the legacy that has defined not just our training, but our **world view**, our very understanding of how the world works, and how we must operate in it if we are to be "successful" and accepted by those we've been taught to think matter. This is our ***narrative*** about what it means to be a human being on this planet. It is a sad and sick narrative, that invariably produces an unhappy ending. Because of our perspective, our perception is unusually distorted. We experience the world as a place of scarcity, pain, and danger, rather than one of abundance and potential love that can be actualized if we just allow our consciousness to shift, stop looking at the world through the dominator lenses, and open our hearts to the love running wild in every nutrino on the planet.

For we have, built into all of us, old blueprints of expectation and response, old structures of oppression, and these must be altered at the same time we alter the living conditions which are a result of those structures, for the master's tools will never dismantle the master's house.
Audre Lorde

...on every continent a revolution in human dignity is emerging. It is re-knitting community and our ties to the earth. So we do have a choice. We can choose death; or we can choose life.   Frances Moore Lappé

Peace is often presented as a noble goal to be pursued. That goal is only valid if we recognize an expanded meaning within the context of Lappé's revolution.

Peace is not just the absence of conflict or the desire of good will; it is the presence of generosity, willingness, courage, community, and justice.
1. **Being generous** enough to forgive and accept ourselves *and* others.
2. **Being willing** to walk through the fear, *face* and tell the truth about ourselves, others, and the institutions and bureaucracies that have power in our household, our family, our community.
3. **Being committed** to an active, open participation in the community.
4. **Being willing** to fully fight for political and human rights, *and* economic justice for all our brothers, sisters, and cousins.

CURIOSITY

Frances Moore Lappé, who is a long time social justice author and food revolution activist, when asked what she had done that made her most proud, responded: *I kept asking the next question.*

It is so important to ask that next question, of ourselves, of others, of those who are supposed to know, of those who have power. Curiosity can drive liberation, actualization, and love.

All over the world people are remaking the cultural stories that have shaped our understanding, directed our perspective, and limited our perceptions of ourselves and the world in which we live.

> *The most successful remedy for fear has been curiosity.*
> Theodore Zeldin

People are beginning to study the past with more openness--asking the next question. What patriarchal/dominator trained archeologists interpreted as hunting scenes on cave walls are now more clearly seen as celebrations of Spring. Studying close relatives like the binobo chimps, among whom there is almost no intra or inter-group violence and almost no hierarchy, has shown us that our natural legacy may be cooperation, not competition. Many of us now recognize that what we termed as fear and submission gestures between animals, in many instances, are just as likely offers of cooperation.

Our scientific observation, combined with a more enlarged perspective than patriarchal/dominator researchers have had, allows us to recognize that the concept of MAN and *his* woman as the primary unit of family life is a very recent creation of culture that very likely did not exist for most of humanity's time on the planet. Researchers are asking the questions, allowing themselves to look beyond the horizon, each day learning a new way in which our world is not flat.

You and I are part of this revolution in knowledge and consciousness. Engaging in your acceptance, forgiveness, and love for yourself, and extending that same generosity to the rest of the community, asking that next question of yourself or others, will provide you with joy and transformative power in a rippling effect that radiates out from your pebble to the outermost reaches of our pond.

Reclaiming the stories of Mari and Hathor, Tracing the origins of Kali and Alat, learning about the Goddesses celebrated throughout the world before the Jewish, Buddhist, Christian, Islamic derivatives became all powerful, can be an extraordinary, exciting, ground shifting experience. Uncovering the hidden history of the time when we humans celebrated our place in the eco-system, rather than attempting to distort and control it, can be a revelation that propels you into engaged work and celebration.

...this is basically what the modern revolution in consciousness is about: the gradual deconstruction and reconstruction of the stories and images that have for so long served to mold our minds, bodies, and souls to fit the requirements of a system driven by punishment, fear, and pain.
Riane Eisler

It is possible to extend ourselves more and more into and with the larger presence of the world. We do this through peaceful relationship and a genuine effort to understand each other.
K. Louise Schmidt

THE FUTURE OF HOPE

Everywhere on the globe today (including our backyards) our brothers and sisters are taking action to bring justice, peace, revolution, human rights, the end of hunger related deaths, and ecological balance to our planet. You may already be involved in this liberation work, but even if you are not consciously doing some of this, you are probably still contributing. When you buy the recycled product instead of something else; when you carry and use recycled bags; when you carry your own refill cup to the coffee shop, you are contributing. Whether it's speaking up or standing up at city council against the destruction of a park or agitating against the genocide in Darfur; whether you're fighting against putting the waste incinerator in the inner-city neighborhood or promoting a fair trade policy with so called third world countries; whether you're advocating for a cabinet level Department of Peace or educating yourself and your local government on the need to more fully manage corporation privileges; whether you're fighting for women's

I think our communities of resistance should be built like a church or a temple where everything you see expresses the tendency to be oneself, to go back to oneself, to go into communion with reality.
Thich Nhat Hanh

176

reproductive, employment, and education rights, or you're promoting The United Nations' Universal Declaration of Human Rights, or you're educating yourself or others on how to create a ***whole new system*** of human interaction, you are contributing.

When you speak up against the racist or sexist comment or joke, or when you teach your children to listen and be respectful by listening and being respectful to them, you are contributing. There's so much we can do.

From the Alliance of Concerned Men in Washington, DC and the urban farming of Growth Power of Milwaukee, to the Million Signature Campaign of Iran for Women's Rights, The Oasis of Peace (Wahat al-Salam, Neve Shalom) half way between Jerusalem and Tel Aviv, to the Landless Workers movement of Brazil and the micro-lending Grameen Bank of Bangladesh, people are reaching, people are challenging themselves and the powers that be. The impulse to love is on the rise. Have you marched in a Pride Parade lately? You might want to try it; it can be a lot of fun. We can choose in any moment to be a conscious part of any of the activities that help our planet regain its balance.

Transformation requires more than mere seeing; it requires all forms of perception, including remembering, imagining, intuiting, hallucinating, dreaming, and empathizing.....
Robin Morgan

So many of our brothers and sisters around the world have contributed their hearts and their labor to creating a welcoming place, where love and justice will blossom for our grandchildren's grandchildren. You and I can do the same. Just remind ourselves that not only does the emperor have no clothes, but we need to help him find a job that will allow him to become a contributing member of the community. There is so much toil and joy to be shared.

...every person is the right person to act and every moment is the right moment to begin.
Jonathan Schell

MORE OPPORTUNITIES: Having spent twenty years of my life working as an elementary school tutor, an alternative high school teacher and principal, and an associate professor, the lies we tell ourselves about **Education** mean a lot to me. The first lie is that the factory method of education introduced into this country in the late nineteenth century actually served most students at some point in history. According to Colin Greer and other researchers, the drop-out rate in most big city school systems for the first half of the 20th century was forty to fifty percent. While the other fifty percent of the students actually survived through the twelve grades and received diplomas, how many do you think actually felt or were successful at learning most of the material taught? If we use grade point averages as a success measure, there were about 20% (A and B students) who were relatively well served by the system. In other words, 90% of the students who went into these systems were not successfully taught what our culture had decided was desirable knowledge.

> Do you remember your time in high school? Do you remember what you learned in Chemistry class & lab? You were there for at least 220 hours. How about Social Studies?

Not much has changed in the last fifty years except that we have a far greater percent of students graduating from high school now.

The great secret is that we know what it will take to really serve our children. We know what it will take to maximize students' learning, but we don't act on it. Why?

There have been dozens of rigorous academic studies over many decades that all come to similar conclusions. If we want to maximize the educational value to our students, we must have one teacher for every *eight to ten* students. Not the one teacher for every *twenty to thirty-five* students we currently have. If we want to have non-violent, safe, encouraging learning communities, elementary school populations should not reach much over one hundred. High schools should have no more than two hundred-fifty students. Almost all learning research points to these numbers. So what keeps us from acting on them?

> What did you like best about high school? What's the most exciting thing you learned?

You may have some ideas about this. It would require such a seismic shift in the priorities of our culture to stop paying lip service to our children's future, and instead commit our fortunes to this task. As expensive as education is now, we would seemingly have to at least *triple* our education budgets. How can we afford it? How can we help the culture move towards doing this? How might we restructure the way we think about or *do* school as a part of the solution? Besides, since the cultural values we've been teaching have helped create the mess we currently have, what would we actually want to teach? How might we change the curriculum, methodology, and structure? Once we make the commitment to follow the knowledge, we as a community can surely find a way to meet this challenge. Doesn't this sound like a delicious project for someone to take on? What are you doing next week?

Surely all of us are nerved by one another, catch courage from one another.
Barbara Deming

Cost, Conscience, and Consciousness

So, what's it cost to reform or liberate education? To heal the oceans? Prevent war? Establish justice for all? Feed everyone? In response, economists ask the question, *cost* to whom?

Let's say I own some land with a river running through it. I'm approached with an offer to buy my land so a dam can be built on it. The offer will yield me an extraordinary profit. Seems like a simple decision, right? What if my family has used the land for many generations and I'm a strong traditionalist? What if I'm close to my daughter, her family farm's downriver, and will be destroyed by the dam? What if I'm concerned about the local economy and I think the dam *will help*? What if I'm a caring member of the community, and my neighbors will be harmed by my sale? What if I care about workers' rights and safety, and the corporation building the dam has a terrible reputation in these areas? What if I just don't believe corporations should exist? What if I have a consciousness about ecology and biological legacy, and believe the dam will harm the environment, and will likely make things worse for the children seven generations from now?

So what's the cost to me of making the decision to sell my land? The economists are correct when they argue that every economic decision we make is measured by what we perceive is in our best interest in that moment. The real question is *How do we measure our best interest?* There is a cost beyond the price tags to shopping at Wal-Mart or buying a pair of Nike shoes. (Both companies have been involved at times quite extensively in slave or foreign prison labor. Wal-Mart has destroyed countless small businesses and repeatedly attempted to sabotage unionizing efforts by its workers. Yet, it also is becoming a major green retailer.) Part of our revolution in consciousness as we learn to bring joy, love, and transformative power into our lives, is that we are not alone. What *you* do makes a difference to others. What *I* do makes a difference. Every day. Every moment.

Sixty-three million Americans now say they base their purchasing decisions on how they affect the world,....Frances Moore Lappé

Decisions in the marketplace are *always* based on our consciousness and conscience. Consciousness and conscience allow us to enlarge our view of the *true cost* to anything and the *cost* to whom. As sure as I am writing this in this moment, both you and I will make decisions this week, take many actions that will *not* reflect a larger consciousness. If we are rigorous in our inventory and continue to be generous with ourselves, we will get better at it. **Really.**

FOOD

Holy Cow! I'm Eating Somebody's Mother!

Food is the one central thing about human experience that can open up both our senses and our conscience to our place in the world. Alice Waters

When we humans eat an animal based diet it is bad for our bodies; it is bad for the animals; it is bad for all the humans starving; it is bad for the world economy; it is bad for the air; it is bad for the water; it is bad for the land; it is bad for our planet. **So why do we keep eating death?**

Folks in industrialized societies like ours are eating more animal products than ever. Why? Researcher and activist, John Robbins (whose father co-founded Baskin & Robbins Ice Cream) spells out some of the reasons.

It is all very simple.
1. The whole show is a charade. It is a game based on repression and untruth.
2. Awareness is bad for the meat business.
3. Conscience is bad for the meat business.
4. Sensitivity is bad for the meat business.
5. **Denial***, however, the meat business finds indispensable.*

I have waited to almost the end of the book to address this issue because food intake is such a fundamental part of our lives. People can mess with how our cars are put together. They can change how we get our electricity. They can cut down on the plastics in our lives, but let 'em start messing with our taste buds and our stomach, and we're headed for trouble.

> *We are all wounded and wanting. So it begins with ourselves-- endlessly crossing over to new territory within; beginning to understand the wounding, fragmentation and confusion; unlearning common patterns of socialization and defendedness which create more suffering.*
> K. Louise Schmidt

> *...lies are long/and lies are strong/When we think they taste good.*

We have been taught from birth that it's okay to steal the milk another species produces for their young, even though most humans on the planet are lactose intolerant. What do you think of when you hear the term, *hearty breakfast*? Eggs, bacon, sausage links, ham--The unborn offspring of one being and the processed remains of another tortured, enslaved, terrified cousin.

Can you smell that savory pain, that tasty terror, that succulent murder?

The facts, however, are simple. Biologically, humans are designed to eat no more than a very small amount of animal based food. In the mean time, *Ninety* percent of the animals that we do eat come through the factory farm system. Most researchers have concluded that those animals are sentient. They can think and feel, somewhat similar to how we think and feel. They feel fear. They feel pain. They feel connected to each other. The most prominent victims, pigs, cattle, and chickens all have cultures in the wild that are totally destroyed by the factory farm system. They are fed food, adulterated by antibiotics, that is not natural to their species, but is meant to fatten them up. They are beaten; they are tortured,; they are neglected. When you eat that chicken's wing, that pig's flesh, that cow's shoulder, you are eating pain; you are eating

If you can justify eating meat, you can justify the conditions of the ghetto. I can't justify either one.
Dick Gregory

terror; you are eating the poisoned future of humanity and the planet. *What a downer, huh?*

Life is better for animals imprisoned outside the factory farm system. If you use local or organic food, it will be better for your body, better for the environment, better for the small family farmer, but for the animals, a comfortable prison is still a prison, and murder is still murder.

(Take a breath here. Let yourself face the truth, but remember--BE GENEROUS WITH YOURSELF, BE GENEROUS….)

The animals of the world exist for their own reasons. They were not made for humans any more than Black people were made for whites or women for men.
Alice Walker

Some interesting facts about food:

One acre of land can be farmed to produce 20,000 lbs. of potatoes. That same acre will produce under 200 lbs. of beef (dead cow parts).

In the USA, cattle feedlots produce close to two billion tons of waste each year (6000 lbs per person). As a result of the imprisonment and slaughter of bovines, pigs, and chickens, ½ of our water wells are contaminated with nitrates. Their gases are also a *major* air pollutant.

80% of all corn grown (after ethanol supplies)
90% of all soybeans
95% of all oats grown in our country
goes to feed cattle.

To grow one pound of potatoes it takes 24 gallons of water. To grow one pound of apples it takes 49 gallons. To produce one pound of beef it takes **5000** gallons.

About one half of all water used in our country is used for livestock.

Up to *20* people eating a plant based diet can be fed with the grain used to feed *one* animal eater.

Our planet is bountiful. If we have the will, without using genetically distorted seeds, we can currently grow enough food to feed over twice the current population of the earth a balanced diet--if we don't waste it by using it to create that thing we call **meat**. Each moment, each of us has another chance to make a decision. Every single time we make a choice, we make a difference.

When the earth is sacred to us, our bodies can also be sacred to us.
bell hooks

As hip hop activist and entrepreneur, Russell Simmons commented, *Like the yogis say, we're all part of just one breathing being.*

He was engaged in an interview with two cable news commentators at the time. They were making the issue that there were a number of celebrities who were espousing a green future, but were really hypocrites because they were seen riding in jet planes or doing leisure or daily activities that were wasteful.

Simmons explained that the criticism was probably unfair in most cases. He essentially stated that people become conscious, *not perfect*. He made the example that he'd been vegan for years, but that doesn't mean he hasn't eaten fish on occasion, or ignored that the noodles he was eating at times were made with eggs. ***This*** is the essence of our healing as individuals, as a species, as a planet. Generosity.

> *Only by restoring the broken connections can we be healed. Connection is health.*
> Wendell Berry

We are all in this together. I'm trying, so I must be generous with myself. And not only must I be generous with you if you're conscious and trying to change your relationship to others, and the ecosystem, but I also must do my best to be generous to you when you're not so conscious. I also hope you will show that same generosity to me when I'm not as aware of something as you think I need to be.

DEEP LOVE REQUIRES DEEP, LIVING DEMOCRACY

I dwell in possibility. Emily Dickinson

K. Louise Schmidt writes extensively about deep democracy. Deep democracy is a way of being in every part of our life. Within, it means an openness to all parts of our self and to all our feelings, all our inner voices (even the ones we don't feel comfortable with). In relationships it means maintaining awareness of our whole self, with all our ideals and all our blemishes. In groups it means listening to, exploring, and experimenting with what unfolds. In community or global work, deep democracy supports political action, ethnicity, separatism, and nature. As Schmidt envisions it, deep democracy allows the possibility in everyone to be a leader because it recognizes that everyone is needed to fully represent reality, and that a true democracy requires that each human being be treated as "equal and integral to the whole."

Far too often our culture tells us a tremendous lie. It tells us that we don't as individuals make a difference .... Your life does matter. It always matters whether you reach out in friendship or lash out in anger. ...whether you live with compassion and awareness or...succumb to distractions and trivia. It always matters how you treat other people, how you treat animals, and how you treat yourself. It always matters what you do. ...what you say. And it always matters what you eat. John Robbins

Relationships take precedence over getting and keeping power, reputation and honor. Rather than conquering enemies one hopes for transformation, turning opponents into friends and allies to deal with common problems.
Jack Ross

Whether we are referring to Riane Eisler's Partnership Society or Frances Moore Lappé's Living Democracy, or Schmidt's work, they all have a *narrative* in common: That each of us can have a sense of abundance, a heart centered reality, a non-enemy ethic that allows us to see ourselves in every other individual, a commitment to a democracy that reaches out to ***everyone***, celebrates our differences, and develops the most useful loving methods to work together in a spiral of empowerment to create a **liberating** power that ***transforms*** us all. .

At the heart of this transformative power is the power of heart, the power of loving, the power of hoping, of wondering, of bringing, with the community, the *possible* into reality.

So, it is not just our individual relationship to the world that matters. To fully reach our love and power, and to play a part in passing it on to others, we each must be willing to challenge and change the systems that have shaped a world of scarcity and fear. If you and I are following the tenets for healing, for being happy, for having and increasing love in our lives, then we each will ***naturally*** join this conspiracy of love to consciously work to create an environment that supports joy and power for not just ourselves, but for all our brothers and our sisters, and our children, our children's children, our cousins' children, and so on.

*Deep democracy believes every human being is of equal importance and has a special calling or **a meaningful response to our larger self and the grandeur of the ongoing story.** Deep democrats arouse people from apathy and make them think. And they often do this more through action than words.*
K. Louise Schmidt

…it is part of our glory as human beings that, even with our imperfections and wounds, we can still help heal and cherish each other and our beautiful planet.
John Robbins

To fully reach love and power we consciously move toward balance, toward the natural rhythm of our eco-system, that has us each as active community members in the healing process of all life in, on, and above our planet.

You want love? You want power? You want happiness?

You know the first step:

Be Generous with yourself.
                        Be Generous with others.

NOW, LISTEN…

AND JOIN IN THE HEART SONG

OF ALL THAT IS.

More Gratitude: I'm grateful for the work of Wilma Mankiller, Mohandas Gandhi, Dolores Huerta, and Martin King, Jr. I'm grateful for the example of David Walker, Frances Wright, Leonard Peltier, and Aung San Sui Kyi. I'm grateful to the sun for coming up, the rain for falling down and sideways, the rivers for flowing, the oceans for rolling, and the earth for welcoming me upon and within.

Look for the new CD:

A Conspiracy to Love:

On The River,
A Journey of Meditation, Celebration
&
Healing

Created by
River Smith & Tom Smith

And the book:

Like She Is in Him
collected poems from a troublemaking,
eco-feminist punk

by River Smith

Coming soon:
A Conspiracy to Love/Power Living Seminar
DVDs.

Suggested Reading

The following books are important sources of what I have presented in this work. This is not an exhaustive list. There is **so much more** out there in new and old publications, on websites around the world, in the hearts of our co-workers, our friends, our current adversaries, ourselves. Like most of what sustains us, knowledge is bountiful. *Enjoy!*

Adams, Carol J. The Sexual Politics of Meat: A Feminist-Vegetarian Critical Theory. Continuum Publishing, 1995.

Bradshaw, John. Healing The Shame That Binds You. Health Communications, Inc., 1988.

Buscaglia, Leo. Born for Love: Reflections on Loving. Ballantine Books, 1992.

------------------. LOVE. Ballantine Books, 1982.

------------------ Personhood: The Art of Being Fully Human. Ballantine Books, 1978.

Byock, Ira. The Four Things That Matter Most: A Book About Living. Free Press, 2004.

Churchill, Ward. A Little Matter of Genocide: Holocaust and Denial in The Americas 1492 to The Present. City Lights Books, 1997.

Copage, Eric V. Black Pearl: Daily Meditations, Affirmations, and Inspirations for African Americans. William Morrow & Company, Inc., 1993.

Deep, Sam & Sussman, Lyle. Yes, You Can!: 1,200 Inspiring ideas for Work, home, and Happiness. Addison-Wesley Publishing Company, 1996.

Eisler, Riane & Loye, David. The Partnership Way: New Tools for Living and Learning, Healing Our Families, Our Communities, and Our World. HarperSanFrancisco, 1990.

Eisler, Riane. Sacred Pleasure: Sex, Myth, and The Politics of The Body. HarperSanFrancisco, 1995.

Field, Lynda. Lynda Field's 60 Tips for Self-Esteem: Quick Ways to Boost Your Confidence. Element Books limited, 1997.

Hay, Louise L. You Can Heal Your Life. Hay House, Inc., 1984.

hooks, bell. Sisters of The Yam: Black Women and Self-Recovery. South End Press, 1993.

L., Elisabeth. Inner Harvest: Daily Meditations for Recovery from Eating Disorders. A Harper/Hazelton Book, 1990.

Lakey, George. Powerful Peacemaking: A Strategy for A Living Revolution. New Society Publishers, 1987.

Larned, Marianne, Ed. Stone Soup For The World: Life-Changing Stories of Kindness & Courageous Acts of Service. Conari Press, 1998.

Lappé, Frances Moore & Perkins, Jeffrey. You Have The Power: , Choosing Courage in A Culture of Fear. Penguin Group, Inc., 2005.

Lappé, Frances Moore & Lappé, Anna , Hope's Edge: The Next Diet for A Small Planet. Jeremy P. Tarcher/Putnam 2002.

Loewen, James. Lies My Teacher Told Me: Everything Your American History Textbook Got Wrong. New Press, 1995.

Macy, Joanna. World As Lover, World As Self. Parallax Press, 1991.

McAllister, Pam. Reweaving The Web of Life: Feminism and Nonviolence. New Society Publishers, 1983.

McClain, Gary, Ph.D. & Adamson, Eve. Empowering Your Life with Joy: A Practical Guide to Happiness Through Mind, Body, and Spirit. Alpha Books, 2003.

Plant, Judith, ed. Healing The Wounds: The Promise of EcoFeminism. New Society Publishers, 1989.

Robbins, John. May All Be Fed: Diet for A New World. Avon Books, 1992.

----------------. The Food Revolution: How Your Diet Can Help Save Your Life and The World. Conari Press, 2001.

Schmidt, K. Louise. Transforming Abuse: Nonviolent Resistance and Recovery. New Society Publishers, 1995.

Sternberg, Robert J. & Barnes, Michael L. Eds. The Psychology of Love. Yale University Press, 1988.

Thoele, Sue Patton. The Woman's Book of Courage: Meditations for Empowerment & Peace of Mind. Conari press, 1991.

Vanzant, Iyanla. Acts of Faith: Daily Meditations for People of Color. Fireside, 1993.

Walker, Barbara G. The Skeptical Feminist: Discovering The Virgin, Mother , and Crone. HarperSanFrancisco, 1987.

Wiesel, Elie. Night Hill and Wang, 2006.

Zinn, Howard. A People's History of The United States 1492-Present. HarperPerennial, 1995

Help for Helpers: Daily Meditations for Those Who Care. Prentice Hall/Parkside, 1989. (no editors listed)

The Editors of Conari Press. Random Acts of Kindness. Conari Press 1993.